CW01072847

TRADING PSYCHOLOGY

Change Mindset Achieve Success

---

*How to Change your Mindset, Avoid Bad Trading Habits,
Overcome your Fears and Make Money on the Stock
Market to Achieve Financial Freedom*

TABLE OF CONTENTS

INTRODUCTION

Success in trading is achieved 80% by psychology and 20% by methodology.

Starting from this belief, I have written this manual in a simple way that will especially help newbies and to understand how fair-mindedness can help you to be successful in trading.

Trading is not synonymous with gambling. Trading in financial markets is not a game or even a hobby. Your approach must be extremely serious and disciplined, above all, your focus must be on safeguarding the capital you decide to invest. Knowing your character, your fears, your objectives, knowing how to exploit all this to your advantage, is certainly an additional weapon.

Knowing what approach Steve Jobs, Elon Musk and other important people of our time and in the past had, helps us to understand what the right attitude to adopt is in order to achieve our goals in life.

Together we'll see how we can learn to recognize our talents first and use them later.

Finally, knowing how collective emotions are at the basis of market movements and how they influence them, together with a rigorous discipline, helps us to get the most from the markets, while always trying to risk as little as possible.

CHAPTER ONE

WHAT IS MINDSET

Thinking by Walter D. Wintle

If you think you are beaten, you are;

If you think you dare not, you don't.

If you'd like to win, but you think you can't,

It is almost a cinch you won't.

If you think you'll lose, you've lost;

For out in this world we find

Success begins with a person's will

It's all in the state of mind.

If you think you're outclassed, you are;

You've got to think high to rise.

You've got to be sure of yourself before

You can ever win the prize.

Life's battles don't always go

To the stronger or faster man;

But sooner or later the person who wins

Is the one who thinks he can!

What The Mindset Is

In order to talk about it and to be able to exploit it, we first need to define what the mindset is. With this term we refer, in general, to the set of conditionings and beliefs that the mind has assimilated throughout our lives. This habitual mental attitude characterizes our ways of reacting and acting in certain circumstances. In a certain sense we can define the mindset as our habitual behavior in the face of situations that present themselves to us.

For example, if a person is convinced that he or she cannot speak in public, he or she will probably tend to avoid occasions when it is necessary to show his or her abilities in front of others. This leads to general insecurity, which if not addressed will become deeper and deeper in his mind, leading him to give up and surrender for fear of making mistakes.

This is precisely one of the reasons why I find it indispensable to know oneself. Knowing your limits, your fears, your difficulties and being able to admit them is an important step towards the possibility of overcoming your limits. Even if they are often imaginary limits that we set ourselves when, in reality, it is our fears talking and making us believe there are obstacles that are impossible to overcome.

We start from the assumption that nothing presents an insurmountable problem, sometimes what is necessary is to have the right weapons for the battle and a little help to take the field and fight.

4 Different Personalities

Will power sometimes has nothing to do with the ability to do more, sometimes it is the forces within certain people that motivate them to act.

The idea that trends can be innate is very striking.

Thanks to research we have realized that people fall into one of four distinct trends: the obligator, the asker, the rebel and the supporter. Each of them has a certain influence on how you become motivated to complete tasks and goals.

Identify your trend by understanding how you respond to expectations. Are you internal, external or neither. Here's how you can use your internal tendency to be more productive and achieve your goals:

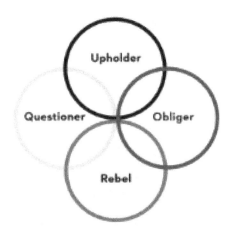

Figure n.1 Personality

Obliger

Bonds easily meet external expectations. They execute projects on time when someone else is counting on them, but they struggle with internal expectations, such as establishing personal decisions. Sometimes the fact that they have tried to change habits and failed brings disappointment and inability to try again.

The obligor needs external responsibility to meet internal expectations. They are good at organizing deadlines and team management. This is everywhere in the workplace.

If you are an employee who is in a working environment that promotes autonomy, or if you work for yourself, you will have to create such a responsibility. Tell your colleague or boss what time you have set for yourself. Find an accountability partner and set daily or weekly goals by testing each other. Take lessons and sign up with a friend who will be annoyed that you will not appear. You might instead think of yourself as a role model for others to follow.

Obligers often think they need to get out of this trend and become internally oriented, but that's not necessary, there are hundreds of ways to create external responsibility, and that's what employees need.

Questioner

Questioners question all expectations. They want to know why they should do something because they are deeply committed to logic and efficiency.

Questioners have difficulty making decisions because they need more information. They need reasons and sometimes even justifications to find motivation. If they are at work and feel stupid, they won't do it.

This tendency can be blamed for a lack of respect or not being a team player, because it seems that they are trying to undermine credibility. Some jobs are requested again, and some are not. Interviewers must learn to ask questions constructively.

Rebel

The rebels confront all expectations, external and internal. They do what they want how and when they want, acting from the source of freedom, choice and self-expression. When someone tries to get the rebel to do something, they resist.

Personality is so important to a rebel. For example, a rebel may resist attending a staff meeting at 10 a.m. because they hate being told where to go and when to appear.

As a rebel, try often to remember what reputation and goals you want to achieve. If necessary, talk to yourself and try to tell yourself what they will think of you if you don't go to that meeting or study that topic.

Rebels also like to face challenges such as completing a project within an ambitious timetable or having a friendly competition to outperform other members of their group. They also love to challenge expectations by proving others wrong.

Upholder

They will certainly be using internal trends to find motivation to act, they manage to meet both internal and external expectations. They respect deadlines, rules and expectations and make decisions without many problems.

Although this trend sounds like perfection of performance, one of the upholder's problems is that they can be viewed as tough, making it difficult for them to shift gears when circumstances change. They also struggle when they are in a working environment that emphasizes flexibility.

In some organizations, the manager may say:" Listen, you need to do whatever it takes to make this sale." Which is great for a rebel, but an upholder wants to know what the right path is. If there is a rule, they don't violate it.

If you are an upholder, you succeed in routines and schedules. You just have to make a decision and then you can do whatever you want.

Our trend shapes every aspect of our behavior, so understanding this structure allows us to make better decisions, meet deadlines, suffer less from stress and burnout, and interact more effectively. The four trends explain why we are acting and why we are not acting.

Meeting Basic Needs

A necessity can be a total or partial lack of one or more elements that help a person to feel good. In itself, however, this lack is not enough to act, there are actions that do not originate from a lack.

A psychological need is not always superimposable on the psychophysiological need (we often find this in psychological dependence on drugs that do not cause physical dependence).

When dealing with personal improvement, sooner or later you will find yourself swinging between two different types of emotions, often conflicting ones.

Some days you feel that you are truly inspired, that you are in a wave, in a flow that pushes you to believe and act; you feel that all your energies are in-line and that you are able to complete different activities without hindrances and distractions.

Other days instead you wonder if talking about personal improvement is really useful, if after all all those who talk about it do not simply live a sort of mass hypnosis.

Thinking positively helps, but in the end you will have to deal with those who get in your way in life, with the long waiting times of bureaucracy, with those loans that do not arrive and you realize that little is under your direct control.

How many times have you experienced this emotional state?

I would guess many, and I bet you've also asked yourself about the effectiveness of studying personal empowerment techniques.

Are these just New Age practices? Maybe just a little more refined? Maybe not!

Between 1943 and 1954 the American psychologist Abraham Maslow conceived the concept of "Hierarchy of Needs" and disseminated it in his 1954 book "Motivation and Personality".

For years Maslow studied different historical populations and the level of evolution they had reached before reaching their peak.

He noted that there were needs that served as a necessary basis for the development of more complex needs and that they led all societies to a higher level of social evolution.

Maslow correlated these needs and created a pyramid-shaped diagram or "Scale of Needs".

This scale of needs is divided into five different levels, from the most elementary (necessary for the survival of the individual) to the most complex (social).

Maslow observed that the individual is realized by passing through the various stages, which must be satisfied in a progressive way.

Internationally this scale is known as the Maslow Pyramid.

Figure n. 2 : Maslow Pyramid

The levels of need conceived by Maslow are (from bottom to top):

1) Physiological needs (being able to get healthy food, sleep, satisfy sexual needs and maintain a certain hygiene).

2) Security needs (physical protection, material possibility to build walls, fences, protections)

3) Needs of belonging (affection, identification, family ties)

4) Needs of esteem (but also of social prestige, of recognized success in the clan of belonging, creation of classes and social castes)

5) Needs of self-realization (a state that knows how to enhance the social work of the individual, helping them to realize their identity and expectations, allowing them to occupy a satisfactory position recognized in their social group).

Maslow's studies began in the 1960s with a proliferation of other research and discoveries in the social field.

Maslow laid bare a concept, which in reality many people already knew but which no one had ever put into a "scientific" form, and it is known that, in the academic sphere, research is only done when observations go from the level of "commonplace" to "scientifically described statement".

What was this concept so well expressed by Maslow?

That man cannot proceed in his evolution if first he does not satisfy the needs on the lower step.

All societies that have not succeeded or could not satisfy primary physiological needs have simply extinguished themselves!

All the societies, initially nomadic, that found a way to satisfy the primary physiological needs stopped and settled in fertile and cultivable areas giving rise to clans and tribes in which there were pacts of reciprocal help and mutual aid.

All the groups that had, within their own clan, internal struggles that caused the breaking of ties, separated, disintegrated and often died out in a few decades.

The surviving groups developed social and city-state regulations on trade, health and education in such a way as to diffuse cultural identity.

And so it was until the development of modern states as we know them.

Even today, when a state decides to take a step backwards by making it difficult or denying the realization of certain basic needs for the individual, riots break out or mechanisms are set in motion that lead to social degradation.

Often knowledge of the Pyramid of Maslow helps us in deciphering our mood changes or rather "opinion" about personal improvement.

Let's take a current social example.

Stress studies carried out on employees and managers of different companies have shown that the type of problems that had to be solved by the group of employees and the group of managers produced, with the same complexity, very different stress effects.

Executives had to be confronted with much more stringent and complex problems in order to achieve the stress levels achieved by employees on average.

Simply put, it could be seen that on average, employees had a higher sensitivity to stress than managers!

How so?

Yet this was happening regardless of social class!

A high level of education for groups of employees, a high level of education for groups of managers!

How could this diversity of reaction be explained?

The researchers started to analyse not only the school curricula of the groups examined, but also the type of hobbies and interests of the different subjects.

And here they began to notice important differences.

Employees, besides work and normal family commitments, did not have many hobbies and many of those who did have interests outside of work, spent most of their time on leisure and purely recreational activities.

Instead, executives who showed much lower levels of stress, used their free time studying the lives of other executives, managers or entrepreneurs, participated in Corporate Coaching sessions, updated by participating in conferences on Marketing Strategies and Public Relations Management, in short, part of their free time was spent learning how to do better what they were already doing as managers!

The aspect highlighted by the study is very interesting.

Executives spend their time attending seminars, courses and coaching sessions to learn strategies to do even better what they were already doing.

Employees, in their free time, occupy their minds to distract themselves from, their occupation!

This explains the different results in their respective stress levels!

Often our days of stress are the result of previous days in which we have not been able to feed the body giving total satisfaction to the primary physiological needs; in these "no" days we feel that we are not aligned, we ask ourselves the sense of positive thinking as we feel far from inspiration.

But how can we even pretend to be at a level that in Maslow's pyramid is depicted practically at the top of the scale (self-realization), when in those very days we have not been able to give satisfaction to primary physiological needs, security, family and relationship esteem, etc..

Managers can spend their free time with ad hoc courses, because that is their passion!

The average employee often feels bound in something that they have not totally chosen for themself, so in their free time they try to take their mind to other shores.

Can we find other contexts in which to observe this identical "reaction"? Of course, in students!

You study to please the teacher, you do your homework as quickly as possible and then off you go, as far away as possible from books and "school thoughts" and it is precisely this desire to escape that sanctions and reinforces the stressful aspect!

So let's get to an important key of understanding personal improvement!

When you feel stuck in life, when you realize that you are living days without apparent outlets, and maybe even begin to question emotions and thoughts that until a few months before gave you enthusiasm and energy, it means that you have descended a few steps in the Pyramid of Maslow.

You are no longer satisfying the basic needs of your body and spirit.

Returning to the initial observation, in this state it is absolutely normal that you have no desire to read motivational books, or take courses to learn new things, instead you feel that everything is reduced to satisfying the contingent functionalism of everyday life!

When this happens to you, make sure that all your basic needs are taken care of immediately.

Ask yourself if you have parked too many due bills on the shelf which are now casting a long shadow on your life; ask yourself if you are neglecting your health, maybe you haven't been to the dentist for years when you used to go to the dentist every season.

Check if maybe the way you eat has become a little unhealthy, pay attention to what is circulating in your bloodstream.

Maybe you used to go running and work out, maybe you've given up some needs that your body now misses.

The cause, however, is never in a single neglected need, surely there will be 3-4 aspects of your life that you are neglecting compared to the previous more prosperous period!

Get your life in order!

Improve each step of the ladder of your needs, and only then can you take care of raising your spirit!

If you do not fulfill the most material part of yourself (obviously with the best of raw materials!), you cannot even hope to be able to take care of the most refined and spiritual parts of your being!

When I speak of "raw materials" I don't just mean nourishing yourself on healthy food, but also on healthy emotions and healthy relationships!

In ancient times this principle was well known by all alchemists and scholars of alchemical esotericism.

Evolution is never a leap!

Spiritual states are reached through the direct improvement of material states.

Matter and spirit have equal dignity!

Do not believe all those false "gurus" who urge people to separate the material part of man from the spiritual part, naming the latter as the higher element!

Indeed, I often use this belief as a test to recognize false gurus from true masters of wisdom.

All the conditions of higher spirituality are attainable only when the material part of your being is satisfied, fulfilled and well realized!

The motivation for all this can be found in the presence, in the human being, of the power of the unconscious.

You can also consciously avoid thinking about your needs, your material duties as a human being, but your unconscious will always present them to you, perhaps in the form of dreams, or physical discomfort or even in the form of sudden and inexplicable illness.

Your body has precise needs that are not inferior to those of your spirit.

The Weak Will

The weak will: what it depends on and how to strengthen it.

Having a weak will deprives us of the possibility of achieving our goals and realizing our dreams.

Why can't you respect your good intentions?

Have you ever decided to go on a diet, exercise or anything else, knowing that it is right and proper to do so, but ended up doing exactly the opposite?

Have you ever wondered what it might depend on?

Maybe it's temptation. You're obliged to revise a lesson from that course you're taking, but the idea of watching an episode of your favorite series on Netflix is much more tempting. "I'm only skipping today, I swear! Tomorrow I'm going to start studying seriously..." you say to yourself, while you turn on the TV.

Or maybe it's your disregard for rules and regulations. The doctor asked you to get more exercise, but you can't do it and you keep putting it off.

Too many series on Netflix, going out with friends, the couch instead of training: everything seems to get the better of your good intentions and establishing useful habits becomes impossible.

Disoriented and confused you convince yourself that maybe you have no real goals, or that they are not really desired, or even worse that there is something in you that doesn't work: you feel you have no character, no personality.

Your goals are right, and there's nothing wrong with you... except that you give in when you should be resisting, thus contributing to weakening your willpower which, as it gets weaker and weaker, forces you to give in even more.

But why does this happen?

The devaluation of the future

Imagine you're sitting in a restaurant: for your health (you've put on several kilos lately) you've decided to do without dessert, so when the waiter arrives you can't order it.

But when you're about to ask for a coffee, you pass the cart with the sweets and suddenly you change your decision, that piece of tiramisu left alone, it's too tempting!

You eat, enjoy, and then you cry.

When the biochemical gratification is long gone and you feel your stomach swollen like a bagpipe, you regret it. And while you're counting calories with your new app, you tell yourself that this was the last time, that it's time to change your life (starting tomorrow though).

But meanwhile you're there, sunk on the couch, wondering what happened, why did the dessert cart get the better of you?

The answer is simple.

The dessert cart is here in the present, while the risks to your health are there, far away, in the future.

You're telling yourself nothing bad's gonna happen for a few pounds.

The risks are very far away, impalpable, difficult to see with the naked eye, and moreover they don't have the gleaming charm of those chocolate-covered balls from the dessert cart that bewitch you like the sirens of Ulysses.

What happened in your mind, in front of the dessert cart, is called the devaluation of the future.

To devalue the future means that the positive effects, which are far away at present (reaching old age in good health), only partially enter into present decisions.

Yet the devaluation, or denial, of the future is only the first part of the problem.

Hypotrophic and hypertrophic will

If you go to the gym and work out seriously your muscles become hypertrophic, they swell and give you more strength, but if you don't go to the gym, over time they become hypotropic, and even getting out of the chair becomes a problem.

The same happens to our will, which like a mental muscle is sensitive to training: it becomes hypertrophic if you train it, hypotropic if you don't make it work.

A simple example.

You say: "Tomorrow I'm going for a run", but the next day, you avoid and postpone it, using more or less refined self-deceptions (too windy, too hot, too many people...). And the next day you postpone it again, and then again, accumulating weeks and months of apathy and reluctance, until you give up completely.

Your legs lose tone and the pounds accumulate, which is not the only damage, but it is only the most evident.

The most significant, and dangerous, damage is what is produced in your inner world, every time you give in and put off.

Your will weakens, as your legs become hypotrophic, and your self-esteem suffers as a result, sending back an image of you that is desolate and depressing.

But it is not over, your threshold of tolerance also weakens, pushing you to give in even to the smallest temptations, those you once managed to resist.

The effect of this vicious circle, often, is the anxiety that assails you when, now with a hypotrophic will and a very low threshold of tolerance, you try to regain control of your life, in vain.

And failure after failure you start thinking something you should never think, which is that I will fail this time too, so why keep trying!

Where to start again?

Becoming aware of the deceptions of our mind (e.g. the devaluation of the future) is surely the first step towards respecting our intentions and forming good habits.

But if we want to radically change the course of our lives, we must make a real "mental leap", learning to see habits as the training camp for our will.

So, running in the morning, for example, will no longer be a simple way to get back in shape, but the tool to make your will hypertrophic, to raise your tolerance threshold and to strengthen your self-esteem.

This new mental attitude will give you, on the one hand, the benefits of the individual good habits you will form, and, on the other, it will allow you to develop a strong will that will make you feel strong and unassailable by temptations.

The dessert cart, will then be there in front of you, small and blurred compared to the new image you are building of yourself, an image of a person who does not give in like a weak person to yet another temptation, but dominates his own life and circumstances with a strong will that becomes larger and more defined every day.

The Boiled Frog

A simple technique to change habits and establish new ones in your life.

To change your life, sometimes, all you need is to change your habits, establishing new and better ones.

I want to talk to you about a principle that clarifies, in a very simple and unfortunately realistic way, the inherent ability of the human being to adapt to unpleasant and harmful situations without reacting.

Imagine lighting a fire under a pot full of cold water in which a frog is quietly swimming and slowly heating the water. Soon it becomes lukewarm. The frog finds it quite pleasant and continues to swim. The temperature rises. Now the water is warm. A little more than the frog appreciates. It gets a little tired, but it doesn't get scared. The water is really too hot now. The frog does not find it pleasant at all, but it is weakened and no longer has the strength to react. So it endures and does nothing. Meanwhile, the temperature continues to rise until the frog is - simply - boiled dead. If the same frog had been immersed directly in the water at 50°C it would have flexed its muscular legs and jumped right out of the pot.

The frog has adapted its body temperature to that of the water and once it is close to boiling, it no longer has the strength to jump out because it has become too tired to regulate its temperature. Does this sad story mean anything to you?

Perhaps you have a fear of change, you've been putting up with negative situations and people for a long time, just because you've been taught that you should stay until you go crazy or that resistance is necessarily synonymous with strength of character.

It's true that we often subordinate emotional well-being to needs that we consider more important. We don't only have to think about our own well-being, but there are other people who depend on us in some way.

But then who killed the frog? It was not the boiling water, but the frog's inability to decide when to jump. If you think about it, you can apply this principle to many situations you face in life.

Maybe you stay in an unsatisfactory relationship just so as not to cause discomfort to the other person. Maybe you postpone the search for your dream job for years and settle for a permanent place where you are bored. Or keep your business idea in the drawer thinking there'll be time to make it happen.

The music in the background is always the same: after all, it's not necessarily so bad!

There are far too many situations in which we lie down instead of fighting or "running away". The biggest fear we have is to change. Paradoxically, we prefer to be in a situation of stasis, which does not make us happy, which does not inspire or gratify us, just because we are afraid of having to put ourselves back in the game. Just like the frog, which in order to save itself should change its situation and jump out of the pot, instead it adapts to the water until it becomes unbearable, because change frightens it even more than boiling water.

So small frustrations accumulate, small doses of anger, discomfort, fear... that sooner or later lead to an explosion. All negative emotions repressed and buried by an apparent adjustment are thrown out at once and often with pain and very serious consequences.

Accepting everything and adapting is not living, but surviving. It means giving others a chance to decide for you. Do you want to resist until it becomes more sustainable?

There is always something you can do to avoid settling down and adapting at all costs: accept change! Be aware that you have a choice: to have new thoughts, to act freely, to let go, to make mistakes and start over.

It's not an easy path and it doesn't happen overnight, but it is possible! Start taking some time for yourself, treat yourself to a little whim or selfish decision: everyday pleasures are the basis of self-esteem. If you cultivate self-esteem, respect and affection for yourself only then will you be able to stop passively accepting every situation and grow your determination to change your reality.

Don't wait for the water to boil - make a decision now and jump!

Static And Dynamic Mindset

How many times have you told yourself this is how I am and there's nothing I can do about it?

How many times have you given in at the first difficulties, convinced that you are not up to them?

And how many times have you thought you couldn't do it because you didn't think you were smart enough/capable/competent enough?

How many times, even if it was worth it, didn't you take the risk for fear of losing your certainties?

How many times have you fallen down after a failure?

To prevent this from happening again and negatively affecting your life, I suggest you develop a dynamic mindset.

We'll talk about what distinguishes the great from the powerful. The determining factor is mindset.

You will understand your partner, your boss, your friends, your children. You will discover how to unleash your potential - and that of your children.

You will find a lot of questions to understand what your mindset is and especially some stimulating exercises to go from static to dynamic.

We'll focus on what distinguishes between static and dynamic mindsets. The essential difference is whether or not you believe in the possibility of improving your skills and competences through constant commitment and practice.

More generally, an individual with a dynamic mindset is open to the possibility of all-round change; those with a static mindset are not.

Static Mindset

In order to understand in the best possible way how the dynamic forma mentis works, it is first fundamental to understand the static forma mentis. This is what we will do first.

Those who have a static mindset see themselves and others as immutable. Everyone has their character, predispositions, level of intelligence. These factors cannot be substantially changed:

"That's the way I am."

"I'm not good at studying languages/mathematics, etc."

"I'm a jealous/intimidating/aggressive/etc. person."

"I can't and never will be."

The traits of one's own personality and that of others, no matter whether positive or negative, are seen as static, impossible to modify, carved in stone.

This is, broadly speaking, the perception of the static mental form:

- Talent is something you have or don't have, you can't develop.

- One's intelligence cannot be substantially improved

- one's character is what it is and that's how it remains.

- It is not possible to improve one's relationships and personality traits, such as the ability to manage emotions

Our motto regarding talent, intelligence and skill development could be "now and forever".

Small but necessary clarification: as far as talent is concerned, the static mindset is not entirely wrong. Each of us has our own natural predispositions, which must be indulged. The problem with the static mindset is that it believes that talent can be judged once and for all, without the possibility of improving it.

The realization is halfway between natural talent and constant, daily commitment.

Faced with difficulties and fatigue, the static mindset runs away, because it perceives them as a threat to its immutable qualities. It sees fatigue as something useless. On the other hand, if one's skills cannot be concretely improved, what is the point of working hard and striving?

If someone experiences a failure, for the static mindset it is a tragedy, because it confirms the alleged and unchangeable incapacity. Who has a static mindset cannot see failure as an opportunity to try harder and improve, so he retires.

And when does success come?

Nothing changes. For some time the static mindset sees its skill and talent confirmed by the outside world, but the collapse is just around the corner, sooner or later it comes.

Just think about the reality of the facts. There are not only successes, you can't always win. At the first failure the static forma mentis risks not getting up again and giving up forever.

In the static mental form you have to have talent and you have to have it right away.

Commitment is synonymous with failure. The static mindset says: "if I have to commit myself to be a good X, it means that I am not gifted/not talented enough to be X".

Static mindsets are often found in individuals who seem to have great self-esteem. Behind this security, however, hides the terror of seeing one's identifications collapse.

Those who believe in unchangeable traits feel the urge to succeed and when they do, they feel more than proud. Success is experienced as proof that their immutable traits are better than those of other people.

However, behind this self-esteem lurks a simple question: If you are someone only when you succeed, what are you when you can't?

At this point you understand that having a static mindset means having an extremely limited view of yourself and life. Not seeing the possibility of improving one's skills and changing one's characteristics, those who think according to a static mindset are like always having blinkers. Where (and how) he is, he stays.

Most people think like that and live like that. Think for example of the myth of the permanent job: the word itself says it. More static than that...

The static mindset present in each of us has its origin in a good part in the words that were repeated to us when we were children. "How good you are, how clever you are, how handsome you are..." etc, or "you are rude, you are naughty, you are not capable" etc.

Other children convince themselves that they are stupid or incapable, just because it was repeated to them several times by some complex adult who was venting his frustrations.

In an attempt not to disprove that "you're smart", for example, a child who has become a boy might avoid starting a certain activity if he finds it difficult at first. These difficulties would cast doubt and jeopardize his intelligence. So it's better to give up and do it now, before it's too late.

It is therefore clear that parents, teachers and educators have the task of raising children according to a dynamic mindset, giving more value to the process and commitment, instead of real or presumed labels that then hang like 'condemnations' on the head of those who have heard them repeated for years. All too often, due to the static mentality, judgments are made too hastily, as if a child's potential could be assessed once and for all. Fortunately, not everyone is fooled by labels received during childhood. Just think, for example, of Albert Einstein, who was judged to be a poorly gifted child or even on the verge of being stupid. Even though we know how the story ended.

It's no coincidence that Einstein said that: everyone could be a genius. But if you think you judge a fish by its ability to try to climb a tree it will live its whole life believing that it is stupid.

You can turn your mindset from static to dynamic and you can start today.

The boundaries between the two worlds are quite thin. If you think about it you can realize that in some areas you have a static mindset and in others a more dynamic one. There are those who, for example, are dynamically convinced that they can improve their intellectual skills (studying, learning a language, etc.), but are equally convinced that they cannot improve in manual work, or vice versa.

Actually, some traces of static mindsets are present in everyone, more or less.

In addition to the labels given to children, it is society as a whole that fills our heads with thoughts that can be traced back to the static mindset.

The spotlight focuses only on talent and great events, which may be the extraordinary wealth achieved or glorious victories, but too often we forget the process behind it, the sweat, persistence, training and failures that came before success.

Dynamic Mindset

I've failed so many times in my life, but that's exactly why I succeeded.

Here is the essence of the dynamic mindset form in a few words. To recite them is Michael Jordan in a commercial of the '90s, after having listed all the defeats and errors accumulated in his sporting career.

Whether you are a basketball fan or not, I think there is no doubt that Michael Jordan can be considered as one of the greatest in basketball history and one of the best athletes of all time. He certainly is an example of a dynamic mentality and maybe it's time to figure out what that is. You don't get to certain levels by accident. Getting on the shoulders of giants, to understand their mentality, is a good starting point, whatever your goal.

The foundation of the dynamic mindset lies in the belief that commitment and perseverance can substantially improve skill, competence and intelligence.

The motto of a dynamic mentality is : Not yet ....

I'm not good at manual tasks, but by applying myself consistently I can become one.

I have not yet learned to study effectively, I must strive to improve.

Those who have a dynamic mindset see failure as the possibility to improve themselves, that is, as a precious lesson, the famous proverb "you learn by making mistakes".

When success arrives, for the dynamic mindset it is the confirmation of one's commitment, of how hard one has trained to reach that goal. Every success becomes a stimulus to commit even more, because the dynamic mindset finds its motivation and pleasure in challenging itself and constantly improving.

People with a dynamic mindset are not just looking for a challenge. They feed off it.

If you dedicate yourself to the development of a dynamic mentality, be careful! You may put your masks and identifications at risk, but it's ù

The price you pay when you realize how much it makes you feel alive and how much it makes you grow.

Dynamic mindset and neuroscience

Until a few decades ago, it was believed that at some point the human brain stunted its development. Then, thanks to the studies of some pioneers like Michael Merzenich, it was discovered that the brain continues to grow and change even in adulthood, due to the phenomenon called brain plasticity.

The brain changes with the use we make of it and if we stimulate it correctly within it new connections are created. So you can either increase your intelligence, or debilitate it. It's up to you.

For example, the difficulty you have in learning something new is a signal that new synapses are forming in your brain and, like neuroscience, the dynamic mindset gives an essential value to the process. It recognises the importance of the progressive steps needed to acquire/improve a skill.

That is why it takes on challenges and difficulties, because it makes the most of them. It recognizes fatigue as a process of growth and challenge as an opportunity to measure how far it can go.

In the dynamic learning mindset form it is combined with fun, and it is something that lasts a lifetime.

The dynamic mindset leads to a vision that tends toward infinity. It is a fascinating perspective, as no one can know where commitment and persistence can take a person with a dynamic mindset. For an individual strongly characterized by the dynamic mindset, unknown possibilities of growth open up.

It is good to point out, however, that it is not enough just to have this form of mentality, so do they believe that anyone with the right motivation or education can become Einstein or Beethoven? Of course not, but they are convinced that the true potential of a person is unknown (and not knowable), that it is impossible to predict what can be achieved with years of passion, effort and training.

The static mindset, on the other hand, characterized by a perennial need for confirmation and escape from difficulties, has as a psychological consequence an extreme fragility and as a concrete effect the renunciation of change and improvement.

To understand it better, let us fully fall into the shoes of an individual with a static mindset.

If my abilities, my skills, my intelligence, my character cannot be changed, then I am doomed. The need for approval haunts me, so everything I do becomes risky because it can show the world my inadequacy. It threatens to expose my shortcomings.

I have no power over events, I can only limit myself to what I am right now without even trying to improve myself. At the first obstacle I break down, because it is a sign that I am not enough. At the first failure I block myself, because it confirms that I am not capable.

Every challenge in life can bring me to my knees and potentially destroy me. From these experiences I can perhaps learn a little bit, but I can't decisively modify myself to prevent them from repeating themselves.

So it's better to retreat and do it now. It's better to give up, not risk it, to stay safe in your comfort zone. It's better not to commit, because it would show that you have no talent. Because talent, in the static mindset, you either have it or you don't.

Learning doesn't rhyme with fun, but with failure.

The static mindset doesn't say "I failed" but "I am a failure".

The dynamic mindset instead leads to an incredible level of resilience and willpower. Motivation remains always high, despite difficult moments. Challenges are taken up and sought after, experienced as something beneficial even if tiring. The dynamic mindset recognizes the value of effort and commitment. For those who have developed a dynamic mindset, every challenge in which you have given your best is a powerful injection of self-esteem.

If I am aware that every time I strive to do something difficult I become smarter and no longer run away from challenges, I create them.

My brain grows and new connections are born, so either way I have my victory. I know that where I am now, in any skill, is not my greatest potential. No one can ever tell me with absolute certainty where I can get to, so if I want to improve in something I apply myself as much as possible. If I fall, I simply learned a lesson, which may have been painful, but I get up and don't give up.

That is the strength of the dynamic mindset.

How can you create a dynamic mindset?

By now it will be clear to you that the effects of static/dynamic mindset affect your whole life. A different mental attitude, that is, a different way of thinking, is concretely realized in a different way of living.

You can choose. Mind sets are simply beliefs. They are powerful beliefs, but still something that is in your mind and that you have the power to change.

A few indications on how to switch from static to dynamic mindset form.

First of all, you must realize that the mindset must be trained in a dynamic way.

If your starting point is a static mindset, you can't just "switch" to the dynamic mindset at any time. To do so, you need to make an informed decision, or more informed decisions, sometimes in a single day. You have to realize your staticity, accept it and promise yourself to reason and above all act according to the dynamic mindset whenever you have the opportunity.

You can begin to re-evaluate the fatigue, the commitment, the difficulties, learning to savor the taste of a challenge. Imagine the new brain connections that are created when you work hard and associate positive feelings to the challenges that happen in your daily life. Instead of running away, go meet them! Take advantage of it and you'll be burdened with self-esteem. Start small; 10 centimeters more every day, and see how far you can go with time.

Think about all the times you let yourself be convinced by the static mindset and abandoned something because it was too difficult or risky, what would have happened if you had acted according to the dynamic mindset?

The shift from static to dynamic can have a huge impact on your life.

What would your life be like if you didn't let yourself down at first?

What would it be like if you learned to really appreciate the value of commitment?

If you faced every obstacle as a game in which the development of your intelligence and skills is at stake?

How much would it change things?

How much better would you feel?

How far could you go?

Maybe you would stop thinking of yourself as a powerful-being and abandon the labels and regrets of the past to create a successful reality one piece at a time.

Develop a dynamic mindset, start today.

CHAPTER TWO

MINDSET FOR SUCCESS

Start By Thinking At The End!

Start by thinking at the end: what is the meaning of this sentence?

Maybe you'll ask yourself, very pragmatically, how can I think of the end if I still have to think of the beginning?

Instead, just by thinking about the end, you will be able to plan the beginning, and also the route. And I want to talk to you about the meaning of that, not in relation to a specific goal, but to the purpose of your life.

The meaning of this sentence is in fact to make every day of our life contribute, in an active way, to the vision we have of our own life: to understand where we are and to make sure that the steps we take are in the right direction.

It is in fact very easy in life, to end up trapped in the wrong activities, in activities that are an end in themselves, to work harder and harder to achieve a success that we discover is not ours: it is very common to be very busy, without being effective.

This principle is at the basis of personal leadership: to define what our values and rules are, from which our goals arise, to achieve which commitment and discipline are needed.

We often see people who, in their lives, struggle and strive for higher incomes, greater skills or recognition, totally committing their energies to discover that in achieving these, they have become deaf and blind to the things that actually matter most, and which are now irremediably lost.

It is instead completely different if you are aware of what is important to you, and keeping this in mind, you behave every day to be and to really do what matters most.

To make you understand the meaning of all this, I often do an exercise (taken from "The 7 rules for success" by S. Covey), which today I propose to you as well. I'll try to get you into the right frame of mind as much as possible, even though I'm not there in person, to make you feel the necessary emotions.

Before you start get a pen and a piece of paper, which you will need later on.

Find a place where you can be alone, with no one and nothing to disturb or interrupt you. Clear your mind of all thoughts and concentrate on what I say.

Start breathing deeply and slowly: inhale and exhale, and as you do so feel a sense of relaxation and your mind become more and more free with every breath you take.

Imagine now seeing yourself on your way to a funeral for someone close to you. You're driving your car, you arrive, you park and you get out of your car. As you enter the building you see flowers, in the hallway you see the faces of friends and family. You feel the pain you share with them for the loss, but also the joy of knowing the deceased.

You enter the funeral chamber, look at the casket and suddenly you come face to face with yourself.

That's your funeral, five years from now. All those people have come to testify their feelings of love and appreciation for you and what you have done in your life.

Sit down and wait for the ceremony to begin, read the program and find that there will be four people talking. A relative: son or parent, brother, sister, nephew, who have come from all over the world for the occasion; a colleague of yours, a member of the association you belonged to and your best friend.

Now think and think: what would you like each of these people to say about you and your life? What kind of husband, wife, father or mother would you like to appear through their words? What kind of son, daughter, friend or colleague? Look closely at the faces of the people present: how would you like to have influenced their lives?

Now, take a few minutes to write down your feelings on paper.

If you have become very involved in this visualization, you will have touched on what your deepest values are. That they are the guide to your life's purpose.

So, always start thinking about the end.

How To Find Your Talent

All your life, you've been instilled with certain ideas, but it's time to take a step back and rethink your talents. A person can have artistic, technical, mental, physical, personal or social talent. You can be an introverted talented person, or an extrovert talented person. This talent of yours doesn't have to be profitable, useful or conventional, but it will always belong to you, it will be an integral part of your personality. Learning to properly search for your talents and cultivate them, turning them into concrete skills and abilities, are actions that require more than just a little effort. However, doing it creatively will allow you to explore natural abilities and discover innate talents.

Discover Your Talents

Stop waiting for these talents to magically appear on their own. If you don't try playing guitar, how can you be sure you can't? The same goes for didgeridoos, knitting, badminton and tuvano singing. Find an activity you think is cool and find out everything there is to know about it. Find out what it requires and if you have the right skills to do it. Remember, who doesn't take risks doesn't win. You can only find out what you're good for when you go beyond your limits and actively seek out new experiences. Take on the obstacles and look for challenges to find out what your hidden innate skills and talents are.

Trying something new once a week must be a top priority. You probably won't discover an activity you are particularly good at tomorrow. On the other hand, maybe one day you'll pick up your guitar and find that you feel perfectly comfortable with it, determined to learn more about it. Maybe you realize that you are very good at communicating with animals living in a shelter. How could you have known this without experience? Maybe you stand in front of the pinball machine in the bar downstairs and realize you're an ace at playing Star Trek: The Next Generation. That's the starting point to figure out what's right for you.

Get out of the house and graze your knees. Experience adventures and real world experiences. Have a go at various outdoor sports or hobbies such as fishing, hiking and climbing to see if you have a talent you haven't exploited so far or a natural instinct.

Try something easy. What is that thing you do without even thinking about it? What do you like? Consider your obsessions and interests to track your talent. If you spend whole days drawing, reading or dancing, it's useless to waste time hoping to become an experienced chef. Focus on what you have and what you can do easily.

If you go to school, what homework do you do without problems? What worries you the least? They could be clues to your natural talents.

Pay attention to what others notice about you. It often occurs that people have insights into the abilities of others, while those directly concerned may not have the slightest idea. Ask family, friends, and teachers to help you understand what's easy for you.

Try experiences that take you out of your comfort zone. Are you terrified at the very idea of getting on a stage or talking in front of an audience? Writing a story and finishing it? Pick up a microphone or sit down until you've finished writing. Do what you're scared of. What's the talent you dream of? What would you like to do naturally, effortlessly? Take on the toughest challenges and find out what you lack to be good at.

Start learning all you can about different talents and skills to see if an activity is right for you or not. Don't be prejudiced. Playing electric guitar like Hendrix seems impossible. However, if you can't distinguish the G chord from flatpicking, how do you know the real reason for this difficulty?

James Earl Jones, Darth Vader's voice actor and well-known Shakespearean actor, has a deep and respectful voice. Many do not know that as a child he suffered from a severe form of stuttering. He was terrified when he had to speak in front of the rest of the class. He learned to express himself well only by facing this fear. Today, he is widely recognized as having one of the most beautiful voices in the world.

Follow in the wake of your obsessions. Generally, what are the topics you talk about all the time, exhausting others? What do they have to force you out of? Use the things that haunt you to discover abilities and talents hidden beneath the surface.

If you're obsessed with a hobby that can hardly be associated with a talent, like watching television or movies, don't give up. Maybe you can intuitively grasp the different angles of a camera and have a natural talent for directing. Maybe you're good at telling or analyzing stories. All film critics start their careers in the same way. They channel their obsession with the history of cinema by studying it and making it their work.

Keep track of your little successes. If you think you have no talent, maybe it's because you tend to neglect what you're good at. Try to pay special attention to successes, big or small, to identify your natural abilities. Think creatively: these experiences may relate to more significant skills and abilities.

Maybe you just threw a party that was on everyone's lips for days. Sure, it sounds like anything but a talent, but if you can relate to others, plan and organize, then rejoice in this success. Maybe you have leadership and managerial skills that will prove useful in the future.

Ignore the television. Talent shows give very limited definitions of talent. If you're not a good-looking person with a rigorously constructed sob story and a powerful voice, you're nobody. And that's what talent shows like that are supposed to make us believe. That's not it. Talent doesn't mean you're famous or handsome or a born artist. It means being dedicated to what you do, thinking creatively and paying attention to detail. It means having insatiable curiosity and turning innate abilities into solid skills. You just have to find them.

Become Creative

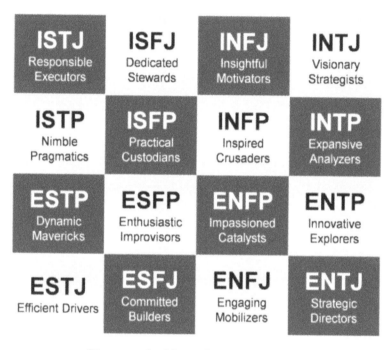

Figure n. 3 : Myers-Briggs categories

Take a quiz to examine your personality. These tests are often used at school or work placement agencies and help you discover your natural abilities. They can also help you find your talent. Knowing more about your innate inclinations towards certain attitudes, ideas and behaviours can help you discover your talents. These tests don't identify abilities per se, but they can offer a piece of the puzzle.

One of the most popular tests is Myers-Briggs, which divides people according to 16 different personality types and is based on Carl Jung's theory of psychological types. You can get a result depending on the answers you give to a series of questions.

The Keirsey Temperament Sorter separates people based on various temperaments, which are identified according to personal responses to different situations and questions. It is available online.

Talk to friends and family. One of the best ways to understand your hidden talents is to discuss them with people who know you best. We tend to neglect our abilities and belittle our talents, so we often don't even realize our potential. If you are lucky enough to have friends and family who care about you, they will have no problem pointing them out to you.

To get an idea of your talents, examine both your strengths and weaknesses. You can imagine that a talent is a kind of innate superpower, something that comes naturally to you and makes it seem easy. On the other hand, you can also think of talent as the ability to overcome an obstacle. Was Blind Willie Johnson a particularly talented guitarist because he was blind? Did James Earl Jones become a good actor because he stuttered? Did Michael Jordan start playing better after being excluded from the high school team?

Don't let your alleged flaws or challenges stop you from trying something new and developing talent. If others have pointed out to you that certain characteristics hinder the development of your personality or skills, consider them. Even if you're shy, could you become a rock singer acclaimed by all? Even if you're particularly short, could you play basketball well?

Give talent a personal definition. Some people think Hendrix is the best guitarist of all time, yet he couldn't play classical pieces because he couldn't read music. If he'd put his mind to it, maybe he could have done. Anyway, many traditional musicians believe that Hendrix was a talentless amateur. Can you ride a scooter like a champion? Is grilled cheese your best dish? Don't let the others tell you it's not "real" talent.

Cultivating Talent

Committed to cultivating talent and turning it into a concrete competence, Ryan Leaf was destined for great success. Great American football quarterback, Heisman award finalist, second overall in the 1998 NFL Draft. Years later, he is considered one of the biggest disappointments of all time because he was unable to improve and go further. Having a natural talent means nothing if you are not willing to work hard to hone your skills.

Once you find your talent, imagine it is a seed to plant. You're off to a good start, but you need to water the plant, fertilize it, and remove the weeds that grow around it to make sure it grows robust. It takes work.

Find more talented people. Remember the saying, "Like iron sharpens iron, man sharpens man." One talented person can help another to become one. If you have a talent or just hope to develop one in a certain field, surround yourself with good people and take them as role models. Be inspired by their habits and their way of cultivating talent. Learn everything you can from them.

Find a mentor who is willing to teach you something and guide you in developing new skills. Budding guitarists need good teachers in addition to YouTube. Blossoming singers need professionals to perform with.

Respect the complexity of your talent. Turning it into a concrete competence will be difficult. The more you know about a subject, a task or a skill, the harder it becomes. Make every effort to get as much information about the field as possible. Take up the challenges to master the talent. Make it special. Make it real.

Playing chess isn't easy for Magnus Carlsen just because he's naturally good at it. He knows how complicated the game is. The more you know about an activity, a skill or an area, the more you'll have to learn. The road is never downhill.

Practice. While you have no talent for playing guitar, practicing two hours a day is a great improvement. A committed person, whether it's a sport, art or other activity, will always end up being more talented than someone who never picks up an instrument, brush or pen. In short, the secret is to practice. Hard work far outweighs talent, in every single case, which always starts with the end in mind.

Try To Be Proactive

Being proactive means thinking and acting ahead of events. It is not only a great way to avoid work, but it can also be vital to avoid certain problems. To be proactive, start acting, accept your responsibilities and control your reactions. By anticipating what might happen and focusing on solutions rather than difficulties, you will maintain a happier and more proactive view of the situation.

Predict and Act

Try to think about what could happen in the next few months/years.

By reflecting on the problems you may face and being aware of possible changes, you will be able to organize yourself and act accordingly.

For example, if you know you are going on holiday soon, start saving money for food or fun activities you plan to do during your trip.

Do not overlook less urgent commitments.

By taking care of normal daily tasks instead of putting them off, you will feel less stressed and avoid even the most insignificant tasks turning into insurmountable problems. A small initial effort may prevent you from facing a more critical situation in the future.

Pay particular attention to preventive maintenance, whether it's checking your car's oil, replenishing your pantry or saving a little money every week.

Prioritize the most important things.

It can be overwhelming to have an infinity of tasks to complete and you will probably go from one task to another without completing even one. Instead of trying to do everything at once, think about the main things and try to finish them.

If you need to organise your closet, take your car to the mechanic and tidy up your bedroom, you should focus on the most important task - taking your car to the mechanic.

Evaluate your behavior to see if it's productive.

Every once in a while, stop and think about what you've done. If you don't achieve your goals, imagine the most effective way to proceed and implement a new plan.

Create a plan, a to-do list, or a routine for completing your tasks.

Identify steps you can eliminate, enhance, or shorten.

Accepting Responsibility and Consequences

Learn how to deal with your problems.

You are the only one who can achieve your goals and solve the problems you encounter. Even if you have people who support you, you have to rely on yourself to achieve what you set out to do. Begin to acquire an enterprising spirit and accept the challenges that life places before you.

Instead of blaming someone or something else when you have a problem, master it and try to solve it yourself.

Focus on what you can control.

There's no use wasting time worrying about things you can't change. Use your energy and motivation to manage the tasks you are aware of accomplishing. In this way, you will achieve much more, and in the meantime, you will gain a more positive approach.

For example, if you are stressed because your child is doing badly at school, realize that you cannot change that. However, you have the opportunity to help him or her study for questions, make sure he or she gets enough sleep and encourage him or her to take his or her duty seriously.

Set realistic targets.

It's a great way to stay motivated and move forward. If you set goals that are out of your league, you will be hopelessly disappointed and lose your motivation as you move forward.

Rather than expecting to lose all the pounds you've gained within a month, set yourself the goal of swimming or running one kilometer a day.

Be a spectator instead.

Proactive people do not stand aside or simply listen to suggestions from others. Act and get involved, whether it's offering your input during business meetings or creating a family ménage program.

Be constant.

Constancy is a very important factor both in interpersonal relationships and towards oneself. Find out how far you can manage yourself and take small steps towards your goals.

If you make promises you cannot keep or have unrealistic expectations, you risk disappointing yourself and others.

Be responsible.

When you have something to accomplish, stick to the task you set and make sure you do it within a reasonable time. In other words, you must take responsibility and give every aspect of your work the urgency it deserves.

Consider confiding in someone all the things you plan to do. It will help you meet your goals and tell you if you can do better.

Surrounded by motivated people.

In order to be proactive, you should be surrounded by people who motivate you to act and excel. If you're hanging out with stimulating individuals, you'll be more likely to stay motivated too.

If you are surrounded by people who are negative, lazy or have little incentive, it is time to distance yourself.

Check your Proactive Manner Reactions

Focus on solutions rather than problems.

Although it is easy to see problems as insurmountable obstacles, try changing the way you think. Try to solve them and find out what the most suitable solutions may be.

If you see adversity as something you can overcome, you will have less difficulty finding a solution.

Express yourself calmly in moments of anger or distress.

If you get agitated while talking to someone, take a few deep breaths to calm down and find the right concentration. Although it is easy to give in to anger, try to communicate calmly and effectively.

Breathe deeply to calm yourself when you feel upset, regardless of whether you need to relate to someone.

Avoid reaching negative conclusions.

Although it is easy to make hasty judgments, it is important to be well-informed before coming to a conclusion. By keeping an open mind, you will be able to think more rationally and find more appropriate solutions.

If someone hasn't answered your text message, instead of assuming they don't want to talk to you, keep in mind that they may be busy or don't have their mobile phone handy.

Put yourself in other people's shoes to mature a different point of view.

If you have difficulty understanding a person's position or want to get a clearer idea of the situation, consider the point of view of your interlocutor. Empathy will prevent you from developing a partial view of things.

If an employee is always late for work, for example, try to understand why, try to see the problem from his point of view. Maybe he has to take his children to school or the means of transport on which he travels are not always on time.

Dedicate yourself to constructive activities when you feel disheartened or anxious.

Instead of being trapped in anxiety or being eroded by doubt, try to distract yourself by doing something. If you channel your energy into small tasks, you can feel more positive and active.

For example, if you can't help but stress about whether or not you'll get a pay raise, focus on something simple, like tidying up your garden or washing dishes.

By trusting people you trust with your concerns, you may receive some advice and, at the same time, relieve some stress.

Ask yourself what or how you could learn from your failures.

If you've suffered a defeat, try to treasure it. Think of the other paths you could have taken. By turning a setback into an awareness, you can take a step forward.

Keep a positive outlook.

In this way, not only will you defend your well-being and happiness, but you will learn to take a proactive approach. Instead of getting demoralized by problems, try to maintain your positivity and see them in a different light.

When everything seems bleak, try to nip negative thoughts in the bud. Replace them with more encouraging ones.

9 Strategies To Seek Success In Life

If you want to know how to succeed in life and work, these are the 9 strategies adopted by athletes, inventors and wizards of Silicon Valley to achieve and accelerate results outside the norm.

In the 19th century, oil tycoon John D. Rockefeller, considered one of the richest men in history, took 46 years to earn $1 billion.

Recently, the Canadian founder of the Slack app, Stewart Butterfield, took less than 2 years to achieve the same goal.

Of course, the inflation of the last 150 years and the speculative bubble raging in Silicon Valley can partly explain this difference.

But the truth is that today there are tools, resources and strategies that can accelerate your results out of all proportion.

I know success in life doesn't necessarily mean being a billionaire, and that's why I'm going to try to help you find ways to be successful, not just economically.

The 9 strategies we're going to see have been applied in the most disparate sectors and by very different people: American presidents, electronic music DJs, scientists, Cuban rebels, programmers and so on...

How to be successful using smartcuts

The 9 strategies I want to talk to you about today are also known as "smartcuts".

Most people waste their time looking for shortcuts to success.

Those who have actually managed to get that success know perfectly well that hard work is essential.

To generate formidable results in a short time, you need to focus your resources on unconventional strategies based on lateral thinking: smartcuts.

Here are the 9 smartcuts found by analyzing the work of hundreds of individuals and companies that have managed to obtain (systematically) unconventional results.

Play bigger and better

Dry question: what would you do to (legally) get a canoe, using only a toothpick?

This question was used during a project involving students at Brigham Young University in the United States.

Specifically, the task assigned to the students was to obtain, through simple bartering, a larger and better object than the one provided by the professor (staples, toothpicks, rubber bands, etc.).

The outcome of this project was surprising.

Some students managed to obtain a canoe thanks to a toothpick, or even a used car thanks to a paper clip!

Their secret? Many small incremental barters of extremely different objects:

Toothpicks > Package of chewing gum.

Package of chewing gum > Puzzles magazine.

Puzzles magazine > Flashlight.

Flashlight > Vase of roses.

Vase of roses > Hot glue gun.

Hot glue gun > Portable refrigerator.

Portable refrigerator > Scooter.

Scooter > Canoe.

Don't settle for a traditional career path, a degree, an internship and a dead-end job in the usual damn company near home.

Get experience in a sector / company / country, learn all you can learn, and then, after 18-24 months, look for something "bigger and better".

If you are a multipotential, this may be your only way to succeed in life.

Find a mentor who has this trait...

To be the best you'll need to go to school with the best.

How many times have you heard that sentence? Mind you, there's nothing wrong with the phrase itself, let's just say it's biased.

But, having a mentor is not enough.

In addition to our master's knowledge and expertise, we need their vulnerability.

Too many times I've seen para-gurus of personal growth worshiped as semi gods while they hold their show on stage.

Often these characters tend to distort reality and their own success story: proposing strategies that are apparently sharable, but have little to do with their real growth path.

But what really helps us are the mistakes made and the difficulties overcome by our mentors: not shiny, pre-packaged stories.

So look for a mentor with whom you can establish a direct relationship, who is willing to tell you about their failures and how they managed to overcome the obstacles encountered along the way.

Learn how to fail

You will fail.

No, I don't want you to fail, but you will.

If you are trying to achieve an important goal, remember, failures will be inevitable, but not irreparable. In certain situations, perfectionism may be your worst enemy.

Quickly test your idea in the marketplace. Keep your ego in check and gather negative feedback as soon as possible. Propose a new version of your idea and continue this iterative process until you find the right approach.

Fail quickly. Fail often.

Take advantage of what already exists

Think about what you're working on right now and ask yourself these questions:

Has someone else done this before?

Is there a template I can start from?

Can I use something already done to achieve the same result?

You have to be brutal in choosing which activities you really want to spend your time on.

Ride the wave

You know Skrillex?

Skrillex, born Sonny John Moore, is a Los Angeles DJ born in 1988, considered the world reference of Electronic Dance Music (EDM).

Whatever your musical tastes, I bet you'll be interested to know how the young Moore went from drinking beers at underground parties held in warehouses in the LA suburbs to playing behind the most famous consoles in the world.

Skrillex's secret weapon was surfing.

His ability has been to identify and ride two mega-trends that have shocked the record industry: social media and the rise of electronic music.

Skrillex's skill was above all that of "being in the water" when the waves reached their peak.

Most people in fact try to ride a wave (a trend) when it's breaking, getting nothing but foam on their face.

By regularly investing 20% of their time and resources in testing the most promising innovations in their market, then pushing the accelerator when these innovations become mainstream.

Use super-connectors

A super-connector can be either an individual or a platform capable of multiplying the reach of your message.

Think, for example, of the phenomenon Daniel Wellington (DW), the Chinese-made Swedish-designed watch manufacturer which, in just a few years, has managed to establish in a traditional sector dominated by companies with centuries of history.

DW's founder, Filip Tysander, has applied the super-connectors' smartcut to the letter, investing his small Swedish start-up's initial small advertising budget on a single strategy (remember, you have to work hard and focus):

Gifting his low-cost fashion watches to Instagram's leading influencers.

Apparently the strategy worked: Daniel Wellington's Instagram profile has reached 2.3 million followers and the company's turnover reached $220 million in 2016.

Beat the iron while the iron is hot

The smartcuts I'm proposing explain how to succeed. The when is almost unpredictable.

What must be clear to you is that you can only have control over the process, over the actions to be put in place, but you will never know exactly what will be the single event that will explode your success exponentially. The hard work I've been doing steadily is a stroke of luck. Strokes of luck help you achieve initial success.

But it's the ability to capitalize on that success and keep striking while the iron is hot that helps you make the real breakthrough.

Don't settle for it. Keep hammering.

Aim for simplicity

Is there a more direct or easier way to reach my goal? What is essential?

Simplify. Simplify. Simplify.

Simplify and automate your work.

Simplify your products and services.

Simplify your routines and personal habits.

Simplify your finances.

Simplify your work and living space.

But above all, remember: simple is never synonymous with easy. Achieving absolute simplicity is perhaps the most complicated thing you will have to face in your life.

Think big

Average people dream of 10% increases. Successful people work for 10 times better results.

Committing to small incremental progress on a daily basis is, and remains, fundamental for your personal growth, but we are talking about mental attitude here.

If your highest aspiration is to achieve a 10% improvement in any area of your life, you will continue to think the same way and do what you have always done.

But if you really want to accelerate your results and achieve ambitious goals, you need to start thinking much bigger.

Try this exercise:

Think about your current goal.

Now imagine that you want to achieve a goal 10 times bigger than you had in mind and you have to succeed in 1/10 of the time.

You realize that when you think in these terms, all conventional patterns jump, and your mind finally begins to think of new possibilities.

Many of these new options will be impractical, improbable or completely absurd! But among them you may also discover "hidden gems": possibilities that you've never thought about before and that, after all, may even work.

10 Habits To Change Your Life

Sometimes all it takes to change your life is a change of direction. Sometimes to change direction all you need to do is change habits.

I always thought that only extraordinary events could change your life: things like winning the lottery, meeting your soul mate, getting your dream job, etc..

In part I still think so, but recent experiences have taught me that a good habit, repeated daily and with discipline, can give you much better results.

To form a good habit you don't have to pray, cross your fingers or hope that the law of attraction works.

For a good habit to change your life, all you have to do is start forming it today: you decide.

Here are 10 good habits to start changing your life, one day at a time.

Get up early in the morning.

If you can't get up an hour earlier in the morning, how do you expect to achieve your goals.

The habit of getting up early in the morning has innumerable advantages: you will be more motivated, you will "create" the time needed to reach your goals and you will have your own moment free of distractions and urgencies.

Take 5 minutes to say "thank you".

Yes yes, I know: words like "thank you" or "gratitude" are very peace-and-love-brotherly, but you don't have to take my word for it, just try to think for 5 minutes a day about the things you are grateful for: the beneficial effects will surprise you. Don't you have anything to be grateful for? Try making a list of the things you already have and wouldn't like to go without.

Your goals are important, give it another 5 minutes.

I've always thought that to achieve any goal you needed 2 key ingredients: focus and action. Visualizing your goals on a daily basis will not allow you to reach them, but it will remind you that today you have the opportunity to take a step forward to get closer to your goals.

Run for 30 minutes.

Starting the day running for myself and not for others has been a small revolution in my daily routine. I'll just list some of the benefits of this habit: greater concentration, better quality of sleep, widespread sense of well-being, greater creativity. Doing physical activity daily also allows you to defeat sedentariness: one of the silent destroyers of our hea

Complete 3 important activities before 11 am.

What goals could you achieve if you could complete 3 important activities every day? Making a habit of doing 3 important activities for you before 11am will allow you to increase your productivity and make a few more dreams come true.

Make 3 healthy meals.

You are what you eat. I think food education is a real life-saving habit.

Record expenses over 10$.

If your goal is to make money, one of the first things to learn is to save money. Make a note of every expense you make, you'll be more aware of your flows. I know that the habit of saving has little charm: we all want to make money fast and easy, but to build a capital the first step is to save: if at 18 years old you started saving $ 200 per month, reinvesting them with a return of 2% per month, you know how much your capital would amount to at 37 years old?

Describe your day in 5 lines.

Having a diary is an extraordinary habit. Writing down daily your thoughts, ideas, problems, results has countless benefits: writing helps you free your mind, rereading what you write helps you understand what didn't work and what worked in the past, writing about your goals and your progress gives you motivation and focus. For my diary, trying never to write more than 5 lines: the effort of synthesis helps me to clarify.

Give yourself an hour.

To give your best you have to be able to recharge daily. Many aspects of our life have the rhythm of breathing: there is a moment to exhale (work, give to others, train, engage) and there is a moment to breathe in (rest, relax, take care of yourself). After an intense day of work it's time to inhale, dedicating 1 hour to yourself: to think, to dedicate yourself to your hobby, to enjoy yourself. There is no better habit to find happiness every day.

Read for 30 minutes before you fall asleep.

I have always thought reading was synonymous with growth. Reading allows you to acquire new knowledge, train your mind and improve written and oral communication. It takes 30 minutes every day to read 20-30 books a year. Using fast reading techniques you could reach more than 100. What would your life be like if you could apply even 1 idea for every book you read in your daily life?

Don't worry, no one is asking you to form these habits all at once, that would be a huge mistake!

The secret to revolutionizing our lives is to start making one small change at a time, without ever stopping.

How To Eliminate A Bad Habit

How to eliminate a bad habit and create a good one.

A habit is a choice that we made a long time ago and that has taken root in our minds. With the right tools we can learn to make better choices.

Habits are in fact the starting point, the foundation and the elementary bricks on which we can build our personal revolution.

Try to imagine for a moment what your days would be like if you could stop smoking, start eating healthily, stop procrastinating. And that's not all. Imagine what those same days would be like if you could get up early in the morning, train constantly, work productively. How different would your life be? How much satisfaction would you feel for yourself? What goals could you achieve?

The magic formula to change a habit doesn't exist. Yes, you read it right. There is no magic formula that will allow you to change your damn habits overnight. Each individual is unique, as is the set of habits that characterize their behavior.

The fact that there is no single magic formula, does not mean that there can't be a general model that helps us understand how a habit works and which are the levers on which to act to create, change or eliminate it. This model exists and is known as the signal - routine - gratification model.

The signal - routine - gratification model

In the late 1990s, researchers at MIT discovered a neurological mechanism underlying our habits. This mechanism consists of 3 essential elements: signal, routine and gratification.

The signal is a particular environmental condition that pushes our brain to activate "autopilot" making us create a habit without realizing it. Classic examples of signals can be: an emotional condition (e.g. boredom), time of day, a physical place, etc.

Routine is what we do automatically when the signal occurs. A routine can be physical, i.e. we perform certain actions, mental, i.e. we have specific thoughts, or emotional, i.e. we feel certain emotions.

The gratification is what strengthens a habit in our brain. Thanks to a biochemical reaction where we tend to remember things that made us feel pleasure (and avoid what caused us pain), a reward could be the solution to strengthen a habit in your brain.

To make you better understand what I'm talking about I'll tell you an example. In the past, every morning, as soon as I woke up (signal), I would turn on my iPhone to check my e-mail (routine) and I would feel a subtle form of satisfaction when I received a new message (gratification).

Eliminate, modify or improve a habit

1. Identify the routine

The first key step to achieving any change is awareness. Awareness of bad habits is the gateway to our personal growth path. Start by asking yourself what habits you intend to change, what habits are limiting your potential, what habits are literally ruining your life.

If necessary, make a list of these habits. The best way to understand which behaviors you want to change is to start with the routines behind these habits. In my example, turning on your iPhone and checking your email was the routine to change.

Identifying the routine is easy. The harder it is to understand what triggers our routine, and even harder is to identify the gratification we're looking for. For this reason it is necessary to experiment a little bit.

2. Experience different forms of gratification

The aim of this second phase is to identify the needs we are meeting with our routines.

Imagine yourself checking your email first thing in the morning. Resist this urgent need and try to make a few small changes: turn on your smartphone, and instead of checking your email, read an article, or meditate for 20 minutes, or even better go out for a run!

Right now it doesn't matter much what you do (of course, replacing a bad habit with a worse one wouldn't be particularly smart), the important thing is to experience different gratifications, until you find the one that satisfies your latent need, just like the original gratification.

Understanding exactly what need we are satisfying is not easy, that's why I advise you to keep track of your experiments: at the end of each new activity write 3 words, the first ones that jump into your mind. They could be 3 words that describe your mood or random thoughts. After writing them ask yourself a simple question: do you still feel the need to check your email (or do your routine)?

The first time you answer "no", you will have found your gratification as a replacement and the 3 words will help you understand the need you are fulfilling. For me, checking email meant starting the day with a "small win", such as a message from a special person, or a positive comment from a reader.

Well, at this point we just have to find the signal that triggers our habit!

3. Isolate the signal

As for my old habit, "waking up in the morning" was the signal to check my e-mail. But it's not always so easy to identify the signal; it's often the case that the signal plays hide-and-seek. However, research by MIT scholars can help us. There are in fact 5 fundamental categories of signals:

The place where we are.

The time of day.

Our emotional state.

The people we are with.

The actions we have taken.

If you want to identify your signal, in the next few days, every time you put into action the habit you want to change, try to answer these 5 simple questions:

Where are you?

What time is it?

How are you feeling?

Who are you with?

What did you just do?

By answering these questions for a week, you'll be able to identify the signal that triggers your routine. As I said, in my example it was the time of day (the alarm clock).

4. Define a plan of action

Now that you know a lot more about your habit, it's time to dismantle it one piece at a time and rebuild it from the ground up, but to do that, you need a plan! For example, to get rid of a bad habit, we could adopt this simple plan:

Every morning, as soon as you wake up (signal), put on your running shoes and go running (routine), so we can start the day with a small victory (gratification).

My plan : once you too have identified the 3 essential elements of your habit, you will have all the tools to modify, eliminate or improve it.

Objectives For The Beginning Of The Year

As the old year draws to a close, and the new year is approaching, the saga of good intentions begins again.

It's useless for you to pretend like it's nothing, I know very well that you have already started to fantasize about all the amazing goals that you intend to achieve next year: having a model body, earning 1 million euros, passing 8 university exams and, in your spare time, conquering the world.

But,, thinking back to the good resolutions you made last year, how many of them have turned into reality?! Ten? Five? One? None?!

7 steps to making your resolutions come true

Resolutions and non-resolutions.

We have a tendency to exaggerate the capabilities of our "Future Ego", forgetting the potential of our "Present Ego". In the first few weeks of January, we always want to overdo it, arriving at February burning out and unmotivated. This year do yourself a favor: give yourself ambitious objectives, but reach them. Remember: if you are looking for lasting success, many small goals achieved are better than one big missed goal.

Plan ahead.

When you decide to pursue a good purpose, establishing a new habit, the first few days are crucial. If you go off on a wild goose chase without knowing what awaits you, the odds are high that you will abandon your good intentions. If you have decided to change your life in the New Year, start planning your "personal revolution" now. What skills, what do you really need to try to achieve your goal? Do you need to be in a specific environment and/or situation to get the results you want? Do you know someone who has already achieved your goal and who can help you? Do you need guidance or a clear roadmap? These questions can help you to focus well on what awaits you in the coming months.

Identify the obstacles.

If you have set yourself an ambitious goal and you don't think you will encounter any problems, well I have bad news for you: obstacles are inevitable. In fact, it's how you deal with these inevitable obstacles that will determine whether or not you will meet your goals. Once again, don't get caught unprepared, think ahead of time about what the potential obstacles may be and imagine how you can mitigate their effects. Some examples? If you've decided to go to the gym, but you know you'll soon lose your motivation, try finding a workout buddy to keep you in line.

Choose a symbolic date.

You don't have to wait until January 1st to change your life, real change can happen every day, every hour, every moment. And yet, symbolic dates can work. Setting a date for our personal revolution helps our subconscious to set all those little changes below the surface, which will be of great help to us when we take the field. Pick up a calendar, choose your start date and make a nice red circle around it. These little gestures send very important messages to your brain.

Write it everywhere.

Have you ever wondered why it's so hard to change habits? Establishing a new habit in our life requires attention and presence of mind. Generally we need to learn a new skill, we need to change our schedules, we need to remember to do a certain activity, etc. Our mind loves routines: if you break the patterns your lazy brain will get in the way. But we can adopt tricks to make things easier. One of the most effective stratagems is to continually bring the brain's attention back to our goals. But how? Simply choose a mantra - a phrase that motivates or constantly reminds you of your goal, print it out on a piece of paper and carry it in your wallet, or hang it in front of your desk.

Accidents are part of the journey.

If you don't fail, you don't progress. Failure is one of the 5 fundamental ingredients of success: failure is not an eventuality, a curse of fate or a sign of bad luck. Quite the opposite. Failure is a filter:

it serves to separate those who want a goal with all of themselves, from those who, after all, are not so motivated. If, for example, you have decided to quit smoking and after a week you find yourself with a cig in your hands, don't make a tragedy out of it: try to understand the situations and thoughts that triggered the desire to smoke and work on these triggers. Success is a matter of perseverance.

Award-winning.

There is nothing to do, we are machines programmed to avoid pain and seek pleasure. If you learn to link pleasure (the prize) to your goals, it will be like putting on autopilot to achieve your goals.

So, are you ready to make your New Year's resolutions come true?

CHAPTER THREE

SUCCESS MINDSET PEOPLE

Shakespeare And The 7 Habits That Bring Us Closer To Our Goals

Starting from the life and works of the Bard, William Shakespeare, we will try to understand which habits bring us closer to our goals.

Whether or not you know entire passages of his tragedies by heart, you have certainly read at least a few verses of Shakespeare.

Few other artists, in fact, have managed to leave such a deep impression in the history of culture and costume.

Actually, his historical figure is shrouded in darkness, but some testimonies and his vast literary production can help us understand his thoughts and give us useful cues for our personal growth.

I wanted to identify for you 7 habits that can bring us closer to our most ambitious goals, inspired by the life of the great English poet.

Train yourself

In several works Shakespeare cites habit as an exceptional force, capable of turning men into slaves or of causing miracles.

The Bard was particularly attentive to habits that could improve his physical performance.

Shakespeare, in fact, who was also an actor by trade, had to be always ready to fence, dance and move with extreme agility on stage.

Not only that. He had to have a voice able to be heard even by the most distant audience (without any kind of amplification, of course) and, above all, he had to keep himself healthy to face the touring and the daily efforts of a not purely intellectual work. In short, the job of the actor, at the beginning of the 17th century, required real training. Constant and targeted physical training can improve your concentration, energy levels and self-esteem.

Die once

Almost all of Shakespeare's works are steeped in courage, think for example of the epic battle between Macbeth and Macduff.

The English poet himself took several risks in his life to make his dreams come true.

First of all, leaving his native Stratford-upon-Avon to go and live in London in search of fortune, even though he had already formed a family and at that time his father's economies were not particularly prosperous.

A few years later he invested his money in Lord Chamberlain's company, when the public appreciated his lyrics more than his theatrical dramas.

Yet his intuition set him on the right track and the rest is history.

So remember that cowards die many times before death, with the brave taste of death only once.

If you want to make your dreams come true in the new year, get used to taking risks.

No, you don't have to make daring or stupid gestures, but learn every day to face something that scares you and come out of your shell.

You lose years

From 1585 to 1592, before Shakespeare moved to London, it is not known what his main occupation was.

Some scholars claim that he taught and travelled halfway across Europe. Others that he helped his father as an apprentice in his glove shop. Others that he began to approach the acting world by guarding gentlemen's horses at the entrance to some theaters.

They could be considered 'lost years', but most likely it was from these moments of experimentation, attempts, pauses and observations that his talent could develop.

What is certain, in fact, is that, at the end of this period, Shakespeare began to write.

So stop flogging yourself if at this moment you feel that your life is going nowhere. Your path will not always be linear.

Mind you, I'm not suggesting that you indulge in laziness and unbridled fanaticism, but don't expect to have clear ideas about every tiny detail of your future. Do not pretend to know always and perfectly, without doing so, which path you have to take.

The road to our realization is also made of 'voids', chases and moments in which we use seemingly confused experiences to acquire more skills and have clearer ideas about us, our talents and our real goals.

What we must always be accompanied by is not the rigidity of maintaining a course that may make us unhappy, but curiosity, the will to grow, the willingness to reinvent ourselves and start again, the courage to try.

In the new year, give yourself the chance to make mistakes and waste some time exploring.

Become friends with kings and drunks

Shakespeare read, observed and above all listened a great deal.

The words of the people, the stories of travellers, the folk ballads. He was always ready to be reached and inspired by some idea that he could rework and transform into a work of art.

In the same way, an open and elastic mind allows us to intercept trends more quickly, opportunities and people that can bring us closer to our goals.

Try to learn to listen better and more.

Expand your circle of acquaintances.

Compare yourself with professionals who also belong to other sectors.

Learn more about topics you've never explored.

As for Shakespeare, it was some very powerful friends from very different backgrounds who allowed him to perform in front of Queen Elizabeth, getting into her good graces.

Next time you're in trouble, you're going on tour.

Shakespeare's life wasn't all roses and flowers.

Suffice it to say that, in addition to family tragedies, such as the death of his eleven-year-old son, at some point in his career, London was brought to its knees by the plague and all the theatres in the capital were closed for months.

At that time, in order to continue earning a living, Shakespeare and his company decided to organize a tour outside London until it was possible to play in the English capital again.

So they kept the company alive, travelled and acquired a lot of new knowledge.

As far as we are concerned, we live in a historical era where the plague is the least of our worries, but even in our case, there are times in our life when we try with all our might but something gets in the way and seems to prevent us from moving forward.

These are the moments when we realize two important things: if we really care about our goals. What we are made of. Faced with the inevitable sinkings of bad luck, don't give up: change your approach, but keep chasing your dreams.

Ask yourself how you can make the situation you're in even worse (and then do the exact opposite).

Think about what you would recommend to a friend in the same situation as you.

Long-term determination and short-term flexibility is one of the habits that bring us closer to our goals.

Learn and improvise

The era in which Shakespeare lived and worked is similar to ours in terms of innovation in work. When he started acting, this profession was not yet well codified and there was no precise course of study. But Shakespeare opened up his own path anyway. He began by working alongside some actors as an "apprentice", learning all he could. Throughout his life, he never stopped observing, improving and learning from anyone close to him. He would meet professionals of all ages and take the best he could from every situation. He used, for example, his experience as an actor on stage to make his writing career more effective. He would even change lines or stage directions at the very last second if he saw that something wasn't working.

Then came the moment when the theatres themselves changed shape: for the first time they were built with a roof that allowed them to perform even in bad weather, to introduce special effects and to address a much smaller audience.

In some ways, this metamorphosis is similar to the situation we are experiencing with respect to technological development, and all the new related professional opportunities.

If you have a goal but you are not clear on the path you can take to reach it, don't get stuck. Look for opportunities to work alongside someone who is already doing what you want, a mentor. Once you become an "apprentice," learn all you can. And, like Shakespeare, always be nimble and ready to improvise, to correct yourself in the process, to try new techniques (or technologies) and new ways of working.

Make this approach your guide in the new year.

Don't care if they call you a drunken savage.

A drunken savage: that's exactly what Voltaire called Shakespeare. To be precise, he said that Hamlet was the work of a drunken savage. On another occasion, George Bernard Shaw also severely crushed the Cymbeline. And, as I have anticipated above, at the beginning of his career people clearly showed more appreciation for his poems than his plays.

So if even Shakespeare had his detractors and his haters and his misunderstandings, we can be reassured. Let's avoid perfectionism, and let's stop wanting to be good for everyone. Let's get rid of the obsession with other people's judgment. You know what's really crucial to making your dreams come true? Not everyone's applause, but the support of true fans of your work and your self-respect.

Benjamin Franklin And His 13 Virtues

13 virtues of the American inventor and politician that will help you improve your quality of life.

Besides being the big face printed on $100 bills, Benjamin Franklin was an American scientist and politician. He was a journalist, publicist, author, philanthropist, abolitionist, diplomat, inventor and was among the protagonists of the American Revolution. Franklin is best known for his experiments with electricity and the idea of establishing summer time, and is also known as one of the founding fathers of the United States.

Benjamin Franklin was therefore a multifaceted genius and, as his autobiography shows, dedicated many years of his life to the search for "moral perfection". In 1726, during a ship voyage from London to Philadelphia, he devised a system of 13 virtues to perfect his moral conduct. The system was based on a precise pattern, which Franklin followed for many years, until the natural assimilation of the 13 virtues.

Each year Franklin committed himself to discipline each virtue for a week, recording each transgression on a chart. At the end of the first 13-week cycle, Franklin repeated his virtuous path, for a total of 4 times during the year.

Although almost three centuries have passed, Franklin's 13 virtues remain a source of inspiration and I thought I would share them with you as a stimulus to start the new year in the best possible way.

Temperance

Don't eat to your fill and don't drink until you're euphoric. Healthy eating is one of my New Year's focuses.

Quiet

Do not speak except to benefit yourself or others. Avoid futile speeches. Practicing silence is not only an interesting technique to develop one's willpower, but in general it can be a simple meditative practice and above all a good idea to start reflecting instead of continuing to fill the void with the sound of our words.

Order

Every thing of yours has its place, to each of your activities dedicate the right time. Often the order of the environments in which we live is synonymous with our mental order.

Determination

Determine to do what you must do. Execute without hesitation what you have decided. What would your life be like if you completed everything you decided to begin?

Thrift

Spend nothing but to do good for yourself or others, that is, waste nothing. Learning to save money is essential to lay the foundation for financial peace of mind.

Industriousness

Don't waste time. Always be committed to something useful. Avoid any unnecessary action. Your personal industriousness or productivity is the tool through which you can achieve your goals effectively.

Sincerity

Do not resort to subterfuge that can cause harm. Let your thoughts be innocent and just and remain so when you decide to express them. Sincerity is an investment that pays great long-term interest. In a country where cunning is praised, honesty is a great virtue.

Justice

Do not offend anyone by doing them wrong or disregarding their wellbeing.

Moderation

Avoid extremes. Refrain from resentment of wrongs you think they deserve.

Cleanliness

Do not tolerate any dirt in your body, clothing or home. Like order, cleanliness is a virtue to be leveraged to make important changes in one's life.

Tranquility

Do not fret over trivialities or common and inevitable accidents. Focusing only on what we are in control of can be a lesson as difficult to learn as it is rewarding.

Chastity

Engage rarely, only to maintain health or procreate, never to satiate yourself, to weaken or impair your or others' peace or reputation. Well, some of Benjamin's virtues can be derogated from!

Humility

Imitate Jesus and Socrates and you can't go wrong!

Steve Jobs: Willpower And How To Increase It

A simple and effective method to increase your willpower.

Black turtleneck, Levi's model 501 jeans and New Balance sports shoes. For more than a decade this has been Steve Jobs' uniform in the vast majority of his public appearances.

As Isaacson says in his biography "Steve Jobs", behind this eccentric stylistic choice was the desire to create a look immediately recognizable by Apple fans.

But that's not the only motivation.

In 1998 Jobs ordered more than 100 identical black turtlenecks from Japanese designer Issey Miyake for another reason. A reason that has little to do with personal branding, but it can be very useful for us to understand how we can increase our willpower.

This the same reason why Obama and Zuckerberg almost always wear the same clothes.

The willpower and the effort to decide

We are all subject to what is known as decision fatigue.

Decision fatigue is a well-known concept in psychology and indicates the tendency of the human mind to make worse and worse decisions as the number of them increases. In other words, there is a link between decisions and willpower: the more choices we make, the more our self-control deteriorates.

When we are well rested and fed, our willpower is at its highest level. This "mental battery", however, tends to lose charge with every decision we make (in scientific terms, we speak of "ego depletion").

Making a choice in fact, even the most trivial one, has a "biological cost", and consumes our mental energy.

That's why at the end of the day we tend to crash in front of the TV, skip gym workouts or look for some junk food to stuff ourselves with. And it's the same reason why successful people like Steve Jobs, Barack Obama and Mark Zuckerberg decided to reduce their wardrobe to a minimum.

Wearing the same type of clothes every day is a (perhaps extreme) way to reduce decision fatigue and keep the will power intact for those crucial choices that need to be made by a CEO or head of state.

Some practical and effective ways to reduce unnecessary decisions and increase your will power on a daily basis may be useful.

How to reduce unnecessary decisions and increase your willpower

When our willpower "battery" is at its highest level? Yes! When we're well rested and fed. The first technique to keep our reserves of self-control intact is not to waste a single drop in the morning when the "container" is full.

Adopt a precise morning routine

If you want to start the day with in first gear, you have to start it on autopilot. Yeah, you read right. You have to try to minimize the decisions you make in the first 60 minutes after waking up:

Prepare the clothes you'll wear to work or college the night before.

Try to decide what you're having for breakfast first.

Avoid answering emails or peeking at social media. Clicking "like" is still a decision.

If you want to take it to the next level, don't just avoid futile decisions, but adopt a real morning routine that loads you with energy every day. The best way to do it? Dedicate the first 60' minutes of your day to the so-called sacred hour.

Use checklists

Whatever our work, we will always have to deal with routine activities. The absolute worst are those that have a weekly, monthly or quarterly frequency.

In fact, however repetitive, these activities require us each time to decide exactly what we have to do, how we have to do it, by when we have to do it, etc..

In light of what we have seen so far, this is a useless waste of our mental energy.

How can we avoid it?! By using checklists.

Define for each of your routine activities a precise checklist (sequence of activities) of things to do. Write your checklist only once and then forget about it until you have to take it out to complete that administrative hassle for the umpteenth time.

If you are a freelancer or entrepreneur, remember that defining your checklists is the first essential step in delegating these activities to your employees.

Establish your meals

There is a close link between diet and willpower. As we have seen, the decisions we make during the day tend to consume our physical energies. And guess what level is our "mental battery" just before a meal, below zero!

That's why, no matter how hard we try to follow our blessed diet, when we are hungry and have to choose between a healthy salad and a bowl of spaghetti amatriciana, our brain will automatically lean towards the latter.

A good strategy to avoid this is to plan meals in advance.

This also applies when we eat at home: instead of opening the fridge and raiding it at the first sign of hunger, decide your meals for the next 3-4 days and shop at the supermarket exclusively for these meals. You'll waste less time shopping, waste less money, and improve your figure.

We hate to feel caged in daily routines and for this reason we defend the freedom to make rather futile decisions, which give us an illusion of freedom, creativity and independence. At the same time, however, without realizing it, we find ourselves constantly caged in an existence that does not belong to us, but we do not find the time and we do not have the mental energy to make the really important decisions that can revolutionize our lives.

Let's be clear, no one wants to impose extreme behaviour like Steve Jobs. Testing and putting into practice the 3 strategies I suggested (morning routine, checklist, meal planning) will certainly not hurt you.

If you do it for yourself, you will have learned something new about yourself.

If, on the contrary, these small changes succeed in releasing even a gram of the mental energy needed to pursue your most ambitious goals, well... I'd say it will be worth it.

Who knows, maybe in a few months, instead of wasting time deciding which filter to use on Instagram, you'll start thinking about who you really want to be 5 years from now, but more importantly, you'll have the will power to become that person.

Elon Musk - How Your Mindset Determines Your Destiny

Elon Musk is more unique than rare.

A genius, many say. One who makes the impossible possible, one who proved that all those who told him "it can't be done" and "you'll never make it" were wrong.

But is it Elon Musk's skill, the fruit of his genius, that is impossible to emulate from us "common mortals" or is it, at least in part, a consequence of a way of thinking that can be learned?

The moment we tell ourselves that a successful person is a genius, we put it on a different level from us and begin to consider it impossible to achieve. It becomes even useless to try to understand how they do it, because we keep it as an implication that we could never do the same.

I think this is a mistake. And if it is true that you may never become a billionaire-inventor-philanthropist, it is true that there is so much to learn by observing others.

New information allows us to improve ourselves in ways we never even imagined. Instead of saying "he's a genius" and closing it there, I prefer to ask the question: what is there to learn?

Elon Musk was born in South Africa and did not have a simple childhood. Elon describes his father as "evil" and was bullied throughout his entire school career.

At 17, he decided to move to North America using the Canadian citizenship he inherited from his mother. His father did not approve, so he did not give him financial support and told him that he would fail and that within three months he would go back.

Elon arrived in Canada with two thousand dollars, a bag full of books and a backpack of clothes. For a year he wandered around Canada working on a farm and in a sawmill. Then he enrolled at Queen's University and then at the University of Pennsylvania where he got a degree in physics and another degree in finance.

He was accepted to Stanford for a PhD in super capacitors, but it was the summer of 1995 and Elon knew the Internet was about to explode. He had an idea for an Internet company and so, just two days into the academic year, he decided to leave Stanford and found his first company with his brother: Zip2, which became the first company to bring maps and directions online.

Zip2 and the yellow pages

When he founded Zip2, Elon Musk had $110,000 in college debt and $3,000 in cash, which he invested in the company.

With no money to rent either an office or an apartment, he and his brother slept in the office and showered at the local gym. The only computer they had served as a server during the day and at night Elon used the same computer to encode and build the technology behind Zip2.

In the early days, when they went looking for funding from the companies that produced the yellow pages, the product that Zip2 intended to replace, Elon and his brother were greeted with raised eyebrows and indifference. There was a famous episode in which an executive of one of these companies threw a volume of the yellow pages at him saying "do you think you can ever replace this?"

Four years later, Zip2 was sold to Compaq for over $300 million. Elon found himself with $22 million in his pocket.

From PayPal to rockets in space

Elon Musk, however, was not satisfied. Motivated by building something meaningful instead of money, he found that the technology he had built for Zip2 had not been properly exploited and that the company's potential had not really been realized.

He then founded an online finance company; X.com, the first of its kind, which shortly afterwards merged with another company, Confinity, to form PayPal. It seems incredible today, but PayPal was voted one of the 10 worst business ideas of the year in 1999.

Elon Musk and the other founders of PayPal sold the company to eBay in 2001 for over a billion dollars. Elon found 180 million dollars in his pocket.

At this point Elon could have bought an archipelago in some Pacific nation and lived on margaritas and beaches for the rest of his life.

Instead, he founded SpaceX, a rocket company to go into space.

Even his closest friends feared he'd gone mad.

SpaceX and Tesla

Everyone told him it wouldn't work. Only a government, with billions in public money at its disposal, could go into orbit. To try to convince him to give up, one of his closest friends made him watch a medley of exploding rockets.

A year later he co-founded Tesla, an electric car company with the mission of accelerating the world's transition to renewable energy, what Elon Musk believes to be the biggest problem of the century. The idea of an electric car was rejected by the entire automotive industry as stupid and impossible at the time.

Today SpaceX is worth over $30 billion, launching the most powerful rocket into space and the only rocket that can land and be reused. On May 31 this year (2020), Crew Dragon brought its first two astronauts to the International Space Station.

SpaceX is now building Starlink, the largest constellation of satellites ever launched, and Starship, an even bigger, low-cost, fully reusable rocket with the ambition to land on Mars within a few years.

Tesla today is worth over $100 billion, has four factories, about 50,000 employees, and is pushing the entire automotive industry towards electrification.

Elon Musk hasn't stopped

Since SpaceX and Tesla apparently weren't enough, Elon founded two more companies. One is The Boring Company, which Elon founded in 2016 because he was fed up with the hellish traffic in Los Angeles, and which aims to cut the cost of building mass transit tunnels. The other is Neuralink, a company that aims to combine brain and computer, initially to cure diseases such as Alzheimer's, but in the long run to avert the danger that general artificial intelligence makes humanity irrelevant...

You can see why Jon Favreau sent Robert Downey Jr. to Elon Musk to get inspiration before shooting the first Iron Man movie!

The "how" and the "why"

The real question in all this is not only "how does he do it?" but also "why does he do it?".

These incredible results did not come without difficulty. Tesla risked bankruptcy in 2008, 2009, 2013 and 2018. The first three SpaceX launches failed and the company almost died in 2008, when

Elon had to invest everything he had to hope to save the companies and risked losing everything.

To stay behind both companies Elon Musk works 80 hours a week with peaks over 100 hours a week when there are problems. Recently, during an interview, he said that the last time he took a whole week off was in 2000, when he almost died of malaria and there was no Internet connection in the hospital.

How does he do everything he does? And why doesn't he buy a ranch in Texas and just play golf instead of going on and on?

The Meaning

What motivates him?

Looking at his actions, the answer is obvious: the meaning. In several interviews he spoke about how as a boy he had a moment of crisis in which he wondered what the meaning of life was. He read Nietzsche and Schopenhauer, but the book that gave him the answer was The Hitchhiker's Guide to the Galaxy. The philosophical content of the book is that the hardest thing to find is not the answer, but the question. Once the question is expressed correctly, the answer is the easiest part.

"We know that the answer is the Universe. What is the question?" - Elon Musk

The search for demand cannot exist without human consciousness and awareness, so humanity must be protected and made as capable as possible of expanding its knowledge.

Why do you get up in the morning? Why do you want to live? Life cannot be just a series of problems to solve.

Actions follow the meaning

Elon Musk's actions make perfect sense if you understand the motivation behind his reasoning. Tesla serves to solve climate change and thus protect the future of humanity. SpaceX is necessary for humanity to one day go "out there among the stars" looking for questions and answers.

"I'm not trying to be anyone's savior. I just want to get up in the morning and not be sad." - Elon Musk

There is a lot of talk about motivation and living one's existence to the fullest, but the key to doing so is meaning. If what you do has no meaning, why should you get up in the morning?

It's easy to say "well yes, but he's a billionaire", the harder it is to imagine dedicating yourself body and soul to something. This involves risk, hard work and a plethora of critics who rejoice when you fail.

Why should you come forward? Because what gives satisfaction is not comfort, but meaning, and meaning lies through action.

Elon Musk is an extreme example. Meaning does not have to be as ambitious as "bringing life to another planet. The size of the purpose does not matter, as long as there is a purpose.

Reasoning from the first principles

Yeah, all right, but how does he do it?

A lot of people have asked him over the years. One of the answers Elon gives is that people don't think about the first principles, but by analogy. Instead of going to the essence of things and going back to the reasoning from there, people tend to take the shortcut of analogy: others do that, I've always done that, everyone agrees that you have to do that and so I do that too.

Reasoning by analogy is very useful in everyday life because it allows you to do the right thing without wasting time thinking about it. Why do you wear underwear when you get dressed? You've been taught to do that, everyone does that, so you do that too. But it's not like you've been there thinking and analyzing the reasons why you have to wear underwear and whether underwear is actually the ideal way to get the result. When you want to do something, copy from others and then make small adjustments to your personal needs.

Reasoning by analogy vs. reasoning from the first principles

Reasoning by analogy saves time and energy. You wouldn't be able to get to the end of the day without this shortcut, but it only works well when the problem has already been experienced by others and there is therefore a reliable collective wisdom to draw on.

But when you want to do something for the first time, when you are the pioneer and face the unknown, thinking by analogy fails miserably.

How can you build a plane in a world where no plane has ever flown? If you think by analogy you'll think it's impossible, because no one has ever done it.

Rocket landings

When Elon Musk decided to produce a rocket capable of landing after it had been launched rather than being dropped like any other rocket, even NASA engineers said he was a fool and would never succeed.

They reasoned by analogy: given the rockets available, given the technology and restrictions, making a reusable rocket would be impossible.

Elon's reasoning was first to find the solution for a reusable rocket. After identifying the characteristics he wondered if these characteristics violated the laws of physics? If not, it would mean that it might be possible to build a rocket with these characteristics.

Since the answer was that the laws of physics theoretically allowed such a rocket, Elon put SpaceX engineers to work to develop the technologies needed to actually create it. It wasn't easy, and they had several spectacular explosions along the way, but today SpaceX managed to land two rockets together in a synchronised ballet.

The software your mind works with

Being smart is important, but just as important as having the right "software". Think of your mind as a computer. Even the most powerful computer cannot work well if it is full of useless programs and viruses.

This analogy is nothing more than a different way of saying that you have to learn how to express your potential. If you do not express your full potential, it is because your mind is missing a program, or there is a poor quality program, or a virus that blocks your mind from completing an action or seeing a solution.

If the hardware is given at birth, the software can be changed and improved. Thinking from the first principles means not being blocked by your current beliefs and instead determining what you want first and then thinking about how to get it.

Elon is a master at seeing things for what they really are and reasoning from there with a totally different way of dealing with problems.

31 years and $180 million

At the age of 31, after selling PayPal, Elon found himself with $180 million and a question: what to do?

The analogy would have said: whatever you do, don't risk losing your money. Also, you're good at building Internet companies because that's what you've always done, so you should keep doing it. And then you're 31, it's too late to learn something completely new and risk failure.

But Elon Musk reasoned first, wondering what he cared about doing. Another Internet company no longer interested him. He started because he wanted to contribute to the growth of the Internet, but now, in 2001, there was a lot of talent he was dedicating to the Internet.

To increase human knowledge and awareness, the Internet was a great project to participate in. The existence of the Internet allowed people for the first time to communicate instantly and have access to all human knowledge from all corners of the globe, whereas before that information had to travel from one person to another, as if by osmosis. The Internet was humanity building its own nervous system. But in 2001, the Internet no longer needed Elon.

Knowledge and space

If the goal is to increase humanity's ability to expand its awareness of the Universe, then it is essential that humanity learn to travel in space. But in 2001 NASA's plans to go to Mars had foundered and space technology was declining rather than improving.

Elon Musk decided then that the most significant thing he could do was to start an aerospace company and try to change things.

Reasoning by analogy and collective thinking screamed not to do it. Elon knew nothing about rockets, he had never built anything in the world of atoms, what he knew was the world of bits. He would have lost all his money, everyone would have said he was crazy and laughed at him.

In an interview Elon described his reasoning in this way, as rockets have always been expensive, so rockets will always be expensive in the future. But that's not true. Starting with what a rocket is made of, aluminium, titanium, copper, carbon fibre. What is the cost of these materials? Suppose you have the material on the floor and with a magic wand you could organize the atoms in the shape of a rocket at no cost, what would the cost of the rocket be? Really low, around 2% of the cost of rockets.

The cost is how the material is rearranged, so we need to figure out how to rearrange the atoms into the right shape more efficiently. I organized a series of meetings with experts, some of whom worked for large aerospace companies, to try to figure out if there was a catch I missed. I couldn't find any. There didn't seem to be any more limitations. So I founded SpaceX."

Elon Musk's "secret"

History, collective wisdom and his friends told him one thing, but his reasoning from the first principles told him another. Elon Musk founded SpaceX with his own money because he had calculated to have only a 10% chance of success. The mission was to drastically reduce the cost of access to space so as to open the possibility for mankind to become multi planetary.

Elon says if what you want to do is important, do it even if the odds are not in your favor.

This, and the other exploits of Elon Musk, are not only the fruit of his intelligence. The result is created by the way you reason and by your actions aiming at a precise purpose that has a deep meaning for you.

It is impressive how few truly meaningful concepts can change your worldview and make you ask the right questions.

CHAPTER FOUR

TRADING MINDSET

Trading And Emotions: How Do You Form A Price?

How are trading and emotions related?

Price is a momentary convergence of opinions between buyers and sellers, and undecided.

The price is decided by the behavior of a mass of people, all those who participate, and all those who somehow influence the opinions of those who participate.

The movements on the Stock Exchange reflect all the behaviours and decisions taken by the participants, and it is now scientifically proven that every decision-making process is influenced by the right side and not by the rational side of our brain, from the emotions we feel.

It is the crowds that create the trends.

Everything is cyclical, and from each emotion springs the next one, in an eternal movement that takes you back to the starting point.

Simply put, each wave can be broken down into the sum of simple harmonic waves, those of each market participant.

Many sociologists and scholars of group behavior have conducted experiments in which it is proven that group thinking is different from individual thinking: the loyalty to the group and the sense of protection you feel in being part of it weaken the ability to make independent judgments, but above all it becomes very complicated not to be at the mercy of emotions.

The emotions that a crowd feels are much stronger and also more primitive (think of panic or euphoria for example, in extreme situations).

Have you ever thought about the reason why it always seems that the market reverses exactly as soon as we closed our trading operation at a loss?

Experience also tells us that - if we had not closed it - it would have continued to go against us.

The point is that, following the basic emotions, we follow the same fears of the majority, we close the loss-making operations as a consequence of this fear, all together, and at that point when the aftermath is over, the market is ready to reverse course.

At every moment of this eternalrotation we can accompany what is happening in the market with the emotions that traders feel in most cases (and their behavior).

The good news is that there are many ways to learn how to manage emotions, and to stay out of this rough sea, both with a set of practical strategies that help discipline, and with an internal mindset that helps us to be totally present and aware.

The Dow Theory: The 6 Principles Of Market Trends

The Dow Theory is the basis of technical analysis: here are the 6 principles studied by Dow on market trends in order to anticipate future movements and intercept trend changes.

Any attempt to discover the origins of technical analysis inevitably leads to the Dow Theory, structured in 6 principles on market trends and characteristics. Although over 100 years old, the Dow Theory remains the foundation of much of what we know today about technical analysis.

The Dow Theory was formulated on a series of contributions to the Wall Street Journal written by Charles H. Dow from 1900 until the year of his death in 1902.

These theories are based on Dow's beliefs about how the stock market has behaved in the past and how the market could be used to measure the health of the business environment.

The usefulness of Dow's Theory

Dow believes that the stock market as a whole is a reliable measure of economic conditions worldwide and that by analyzing the global market, it is possible to accurately assess these conditions and identify the direction of important market trends and the likely direction of individual stocks.

Based on this theory, Dow created the Dow Jones Industrial Index and the Dow Jones Index Railroad Index (now the Transportation Index), originally developed by Dow for the Wall Street Journal. Dow created these indices because he was convinced that they provided an accurate reflection of business conditions within the economy, covering two major economic sectors: industrial and rail (transport).

Although these have changed over the last 100 years, Dow's Theory still applies to market indices today.

Much of what we know today as technical analysis has its roots in the Dow Theory. For this reason, all operators using technical analysis should know the six basic principles of the Dow Theory.

The 6 Basic Principles

The Dow Theory is divided into 6 principles, all deepened in the analysis and development of the theory we will see later.

The 6 basic principles of the Dow Theory are:

- In the market there are three types of trend (primary, secondary, minor);

- Trends are divided into three phases (accumulation, speculation, distribution);

- The market discounts all new products;

- The indices on the stock market must confirm each other;

- Volumes must confirm the trend;

- The trend remains confirmed until a clear reversal.

Let's take a closer look at all 6 principles of the Dow Theory.

The three market trends

An important part of the Dow Theory lies in the distinction of the various market directions. To do this, the Dow Theory uses trend analysis.

The Dow Theory identifies three trends in the market: primary trend, secondary trend and minor trend. The primary trend is a larger trend that lasts more than a year, while the secondary trend is an intermediate trend that lasts from three weeks to three months and is often associated with a movement against the primary trend. Finally, the minor trend often lasts less than three weeks and is associated with movements in the intermediate trend.

The primary trend

In Dow's Theory, the primary trend is the main market trend, which makes it the most important one to determine. This is because the prevailing trend is the one affecting stock price movements. The primary trend also has an impact on secondary and minor trends within the market.

Dow has established that a primary trend generally has a duration of one and three years, but in some cases this indication may vary.

Regardless of the duration of the trend, the primary trend remains active until there is a confirmed reversal.

For example, if in a bullish trend the price closes below a previous low, it could be a sign that the market is heading down, not up.

In trend analysis, one of the most difficult things to determine is how long the price movement will remain within a primary trend before it reverses direction. The most important thing is to identify the direction of this trend and position yourself on it, not against it, until signs suggest that the primary trend has been reversed.

The secondary (or intermediate) trend

In Dow Theory, a primary trend is the main direction in which the market is moving. Conversely, a secondary trend moves in the opposite direction to the primary trend, or as a correction to the primary trend.

For example, an upward primary trend will be composed of several bearish secondary trends, translated into movements in which the maximum of a bullish movement is lower than the maximum of the previous movement.

In a primary downward trend the secondary trend will instead be upward, i.e. a movement in which the minimum is higher than the minimum of the previous movement.

Below is an example of a secondary trend within a primary bullish trend.

Note how short-term highs (indicated by the horizontal lines) cannot create higher highs, suggesting a short-term downward trend. Since the retracement does not fall below the October low, traders will use this signal to confirm the validity of the correction within a primary bullish trend.

In general, a secondary (or intermediate) trend typically lasts from three weeks to three months, while the secondary trend retracement is generally between one third and two thirds of the primary trend movement. For example, if the primary bullish trend moves the Dow Jones from 10,000 to 12,500 (+2,500 points), one would expect the secondary trend to move the index down by about 833 (⅓ by 2,500).

Another important feature of the secondary trend is that its movements are often more volatile than those of the primary movement.

The minor trend

The last of the three trend types in the Dow Theory is the lowest trend, defined as a market movement lasting less than three weeks. The minor trend generally includes corrective movements within the secondary trend, or those movements that go against the direction of the secondary trend.

Because of its short-term nature and the main long-term focus in the Dow Theory, the minor trend does not play a fundamental role according to the followers of the theory. But this does not mean that it is completely irrelevant; the minor trend is to be looked at with the general picture in mind, since these short-term price movements are a part of both the primary and the secondary trend.

Most supporters of the Dow Theory focus on primary and secondary trends, since following minor trends involves considerable risks.

If you pay too much attention to minor trends, you may fall into irrational trading, as investors may be distracted by short-term volatility and lose sight of the bigger picture.

Simply put, the longer the period of time included in the trend, the more important the trend is.

Trends have 3 phases

The second principle of the Dow Theory explains that market trends have and follow 3 different phases.

The 3 types of trend phases are called accumulation, speculation and distribution. The last phase, distribution, is called the access phase in a bullish market and the panic phase in a bear market.

Accumulation phase

❑ In the bullish market

The accumulation phase in a bullish market is where the upward trend begins, which usually coincides with the low of a bearish trend (but not always). This is the point where well-informed and professional traders enter the market getting the best prices, as the market in this first phase is undervalued.

This is the most difficult phase of a bullish trend to detect, as it can be confused with a simple trend oscillation within a range. The technical analysis can indicate an entry into the accumulation phase, since this phase is often preceded by a consolidation phase of the previous bearish trend.

❑ In bearish market

Within a bearish market, the participation phase occurs when experienced traders sell or cut positions thinking that the market is overbought. Once again, this phase is difficult to detect. Technical analysis can be useful to identify it, as it generally comes after a bullish trend and a period of consolidation.

Participation phase

❑ Bullish market

The phase of participation in the bullish trend comes when the good news begins to be received by the general public. The masses start buying, pushing prices higher and higher. This phase is not necessarily steeper than the accumulation phase, but generally lasts longer and prices move more.

❑ Bearish market

Given the mass participation of investors in a bearish market, the participation phase is usually the longest part of the trend and with the largest price movement. Those who follow the trend usually exit the market at this time, or enter a short position (a short position is when an investor borrows shares from a broker and sells them in the market. The investor must return the borrowed securities by buying them back from the market, hoping that the price will fall).

Distribution phase

❏ Bullish market excess

The excess phase begins when experienced investors begin to reduce exposure and take a share of the profits. It is the trend phase where traders should start looking for signs of weakness in the bullish momentum. The excess phase is a typical event during the bursting of a speculative bubble.

❏ Panic in the bearish market

Again, the opposite is true of the excess phase. A shock of negativity enters the market and a flurry of sales sometimes results in panic levels. Some experienced investors will start deciding to enter the market at this point to try to profit from the bad news.

The market takes all the news

The third principle of the Dow Theory is simple but intuitive: the market feels, metabolizes and moves in the wake of news about it.

This means that the stock markets, the Forex market, commodities market, etc. evaluate and discount all news about the market as soon as it is released.

The market is "efficiently informed" about all news, whether it is news about economic fundamentals, interest rate data, announcements about corporate data, or general sentiment. Natural disasters also have a certain weight on prices in the market.

As soon as things change, the market adjusts extremely quickly to reflect the new market valuation.

The third principle of the Dow Theory is one of the most popular discussions within technical analysis; AT focuses on predicting future price movements based on chart patterns, price action, support and resistance levels and technical indicators - it does not look at other factors such as fundamental news. However, all traders who base their strategies on technical analysis should have extensive knowledge of fundamentals before opening a position.

Market Indices Confirm Each Other

The Dow Theory argues that similar indices should be correlated because they have the same exposure to current economic conditions. For example, the Dow Jones must have a correlation with the Dow Jones Transportation Index. If there is some kind of divergence, Dow argues that there will be a trend change on one of the indices, so it is difficult to predict where this new primary trend will start or if it will develop. If, however, there is a correlation, then a confirmation of the trend is generated.

Trends must be confirmed by volumes

If higher volumes accompany the rise or fall of the trend, this is a good indicator that confirms the strength of the trend according to the Dow Theory. If we are in presence of low volumes, instead, the trend could still be valid, but it is not representative of an overall vision. The Dow Theory assumes that volume accompanies price movements as an indicator. It is a secondary indicator that confirms the price movement, thus confirming the trend. In fact, the volume should increase when prices go up or down, indicating that more people are exposed to the market.

The trend remains confirmed until clear evidence to the contrary

A clear trend reversal must take place before the start of a new trend. The trend usually ends in corporate and economic conditions strong enough to force the trend change. But a trend could pass through a phase of correction of the secondary trend and then continue with the primary trend: the technical analysis can help to establish the signals that indicate the end of the trend.

The objective of trend traders is not to confuse a correction with the beginning of a new primary trend. That is why they expect clear evidence to make sure that the trend is definitely finished.

Conclusions

The Dow Theory is the building blocks of Technical Analysis; however, the world has changed in the last 100 years. The links between all indices are less strong, with technology buying indices that have taken hold in the market and other world indices that have gained in importance. The numerous analyses of the many indices that exist today are reducing the accuracy of the Dow Theory. There is no doubt, however, that the Dow Theory is important for technical analysis.

Emotional Balance And Mindfulness

Emotional balance and mindfullness are the two components for trading success.

In my experience as a trader, having already started to do meditation, I saw that I needed to find strategies and techniques for managing emotions, and then apply them better alongside the skills acquired with mindfullness.

Tripartition of the brain (Paul MacLean)

Neurologist Paul MacLean has been developing the tripartite brain theory since 1949.

The human brain has evolved to be what it is today through various stages of development, which are found in the three sectors into which it is divided:

1. Reptile brain:

This is the oldest part and manages the basic survival functions:

Instincts, reproduction, sleep, digestion, blood circulation, sense of territory and survival instinct, then offense and defense. It therefore works in an impulsive way, and it is also said to be primitive.

2. Mammalian brain or limbic system:

It is present only in mammals, governs emotions related to attachment and social relationships, emotions and pre-verbal memories. In particular the amygdala provides each stimulus with the right level of attention, enriching it with emotions, and managing fear and emotional memories through confrontation of present experience with past experience.

3. Neocortex:

Present only in humans, it is divided into right and left hemisphere. It deals with thinking, reasoning, planning and talking, using logic and creativity. It processes the information received through experiences, and performs all cognitive functions

The discoveries of neuroscience

According to Professor Sam Wang, neuroscientist at Princeton University, information is not only an important part of the whole decision-making process, but it is the starting point.

We hear before we think.

These are the steps:

1) Event

2) the evaluation by the amygdala causes an emotion

3) an emotional signal is sent to the neocortex.

4) here different emotions are combined in a feeling

5) Sensations mixed with experience become a thought

Reinventing ourselves to create the trader's state of mind

Biology, circumstances, the process of adaptation, growth, emotional attachment, and other things create our perceptual map, that is, our way of seeing the world automatically, which is composed of beliefs, perceptions and mental conversations.

These things all together determine the way we trade.

These elements must be brought to the surface, to our awareness, examined and reorganized.

This is a three-step process:

1. Emotion management:

How to use body and mind to deal with emotions, in particular fear, and thus acquire the ability to handle fear, greed, impulsiveness, etc. so that they don't take control of the trading and short-circuit us emotionally.

2. New way of understanding the mind:

We learn to see our inner dialogue, our thoughts, in a different way.

Through mindfulness we can become the observers of our mind, and see how we are in our thoughts instead of thinking them.

At this point we can reorganize the perception of the market, so that the trading becomes a a possibility but not just a possibility. The key is to go from having the focus on not losing, to being focused on risk management, so that the chances of success are in our favor.

3. Align our complete nature to achieve the ideal performance, which is already inside of us.

Learning to awaken dormant aspects of ourselves, how to access them, so that we can permanently reorganize our state of mind as traders. From this position we can experience the calm, discipline, impartiality and courage necessary to achieve the highest-performance mental state in trading.

It is therefore necessary first to learn how to regulate one's emotions, possibly reaching one state of emotional equilibrium, and then apply the capacity for awareness and presence and only then will it be possible to make the necessary changes, reorganize your mind to be able to trade from a high-performance mental state.

The Psychology and Rules of Trading

Trading is a discipline made of pure adrenaline but also of impatience, success and failure. These boundaries are very close. A thin line connects them, more than you can imagine, and this is where emotions come into play!

Learning to control your emotions using trading psychology can make an essential contribution to your operations and above all to your work life balance. Just like in sport or any good student with a good work ethic there is an essential component that should not be underestimated: the mind. It is able to give us unexpected results with less effort over time if we learn to train it constantly without getting to stress burnout.

To create the trader's mind

- Compose your daily schedule

- Create and Organize Your Workspaces

- Achieves goals and not bets dictated by impetus

- Study rather than rely on improbable illogical coincidences.

- Be tenacious and patient

- Don't live trade with Anxiety.

- Don't rely only on your gut (used alone in trading it is practically useless)!

Why is the emotional impact so important in Trading and for those who operate in the financial markets?

The mindset is definitely one of the most important aspects for those who approach the world of Personal Finance and Trading. Success depends on you and the choices you make at every stage of trading in the markets. Learn how to manage your emotions and consequently your portfolio first.

The phases to control

- Trade Identification

- Analysis

- Opening a position

- Monitoring

- Risk management

- Management of profits and/or losses

The first real Position you must take is to dedicate yourself to learning how to treat your Mind like a muscle. It must be kept in constant training and as we said, you must not expose it to excessive stress.

The right mindset is definitely made of discipline, rhythms and rules such as waking up early, for example that will allow you to make your habits a strength and not a weakness.

We don't realize that our Time is for the most part composed of our reactions that only lead us to react to events and not to learn to foresee them. Being masters of ourselves is the first great rule not to be conditioned by what surrounds us but rather to take advantage of the best opportunities.

What are the most common errors in managing trading emotions?

Haste is the enemy of Time

Being hasty for fear of losing your earnings or money invested in an open trading position certainly does not help the management of your savings.

Start from the fundamental concept of investing only as much as you are willing to lose and organize your money management so as not to risk exposing yourself too much to market fluctuations.

Allowing your strategy to be tested truly and without mental filters can be a good way to see if we are on the right track.

Mistakes as Opportunities

Don't see every trade in loss as a loss of your portfolio but as an opportunity to learn the hard laws of the market and make sure that you are on the right side as much as possible thanks to your constant improvement.

You never stop learning, but there is a difference between misreading a market analysis or prediction rather than literally being overwhelmed by emotions by halving or losing any profits.

What are the main emotions to keep under control?

Greed

Greed can make you a psychological slave to open market positions. A trader must have their own plan (better if written). In this case it is also beneficial to use the good old pen and paper to emphasise the points to be respected.

Trust in the Market

Consistency with your strategy should not lead you to believe it is infallible or winning at any cost. Everything has a cost and trust in the hope of seeing your positions rise or fall only exposes us to unnecessary risks.

Being prey to the market is not difficult so learn to be aware that sometimes it is better to soothe losses and reopen at other points rather than be clouded by confidence in the market.

Anxiety

The anxiety in the market stages that we listed before, especially in opening and managing an open position is very common for beginners. Trading is done on the basis of study but also of probability and this leads us to fear for our investments.

There are tools that can make our operations more serene and make us understand that Trading should be looked at as an opportunity to understand.

A correctly set stop loss can help us to prevent unwanted losses.

The take profit instead will allow us to close a trend gain at a given point.

The Trading Plan

Something that can help us to control our emotions and set our daily, weekly and monthly trading path is to have a well-defined plan.

The Trading Plan in fact will not only allow us to go to write the result of our analysis and identify the underlying trend. The market is a complicated environment, as dense and intrinsic as a Forest where moments of greater volatility, perhaps with important news, overwhelm the market and destabilize us too.

The Trading Plan will allow you to focus your strategy and make it as consistent as possible with your operations.

Day Trading

Day trading (or intraday trading) is perhaps the most difficult and complex one to deal with as psychological pressure. It is perhaps the area where the fear of loss can have the most devastating effect. Anything can happen during your trading day and this is why you have to be well-organized mentally to face the roller coaster that the market offers us, called in jargon The Ups n 'Downs

I'm not gonna tell you to deprive yourself of your emotions or put them aside like a robot. That's not what I want to convey to you because it would deprive Trading of its part that you are most passionate about and that makes it compelling.

Always remember that Trading is a business and as such is composed of plans and strategies that will lead you to make choices.

Choices that require real actions and therefore taking responsibility. Being greedy or fearful only increases your daily losses and worries. The latter at too great a volume, even more so than money, end up becoming unmanageable.

There are no infallible methods but only you can bring your personal growth in trading and not just to a higher and higher level with simple good habits. Don't forget to use your Mind!

Trading and discipline

But what is discipline in trading?

Many people would answer that it is the ability to continuously perform their own strategy and follow your own rules.

This also includes the preparation and evaluation part of a trade.

It is therefore necessary:

1) to have a strategy that has statistically positive results over time

2) to be able to put it into practice

The first is necessary and you must already have a strategy to apply discipline to.

In trading the most important challenge is against yourself.

You often hear traders complaining about their lack of discipline.

Let's start by saying that the word discipline in trading is a bit too general: in reality they may be very different behaviors due to not having it, and no one experiences them all.

In general, each of us will have a couple of areas in which we concentrate our major obstacles of trading, and you'd only have to remove those to take it to the next level.

It's very useful that everyone realizes what their challenges are, those that have the worst impact on their own, so that they can overcome those in particular, putting their difficulties into another perspective.

What are the reasons why traders lose discipline?

Traders lose discipline for many reasons, and in various areas:

Strategy

The first possible problem is not having a strategy that has a statistical advantage. Without one, it is intuitive to understand that you cannot trade profitably on a constant basis. By the way, it is not even possible that you understand whether you are disciplined or not.

Another problem is not to choose the market, the time frame, the type of trading that are more appropriate to your skills and aptitudes, your risk tolerance and your character. If you go against your nature it is quite normal that you have problems following those rules.

For example, a person who is very analytical and reflective, who is used to making decisions very calmly and after long deliberation, is not the best candidate for short time frame strategies, where they will excel people with a great ability to look, synthesize, and decision-making speed.

The risk in the first case is that by not being able to get into the operations in time, that person will come in late when the trade is no longer available to be made.

Lack of confidence in the strategy is usually due to a lack of knowledge statistics: it happens that the reason for a series of losses is simply inherent in the chosen strategy, and know what kind of distribution the results of the trades can have, at least on the basis of back tests, can take away this distrust.

Mind

Boredom, distraction and flat markets are a first problem for the mind. There are long periods when nothing happens on the charts. If you get bored you can make trades just to do something, and not because an opportunity has presented itself according to your strategy. Finding other things to do in these situations is fundamental: reading, doing research, studying, develop new strategies, etc.

Fatigue and mental overload lead to low concentration. Just as there are very calm periods, there are other very excited, intense ones. After a day on the monitor with high attention you feel tired, both physically and mentally. When you are tired, the incidence of errors is much higher and your performance drops.

You have to learn to recognize signs of fatigue, to dose your energy, and above all to recover from them as the day goes on, especially with recovery exercises from the stress, which restore your mental and physical energy in minutes.

Emotivity

After a few loss trades you may feel anger or frustration, and these are dangerous emotions:

they cause physiological changes (cortisol production, the stress hormone) and... that compromise your ability to make rational, objective decisions.

Wait until you are back in a good state of mind before making decisions regarding trading, (stress recovery exercises are also very useful here), otherwise you will not make the right ones.

Even a series of positive trades can be dangerous: it leads to overconfidence, which can increase size in an exaggerated way and make us enter into transactions that are not completely correct, because it lowers our perception of risk.

You need to learn to recognize overconfidence, which like every emotion has its own severed physical pattern, so you know when you are at risk and be careful to use appropriate sizes.

Not accepting losses is another big problem, because it leads to moving the brakes and letting the losses run.

Learning to accept them and dealing with them effectively is essential to be disciplined.

Taking too many risks (compared to our personal perception of risk) leads to a high level of stress, therefore anxiety and worry, which compromise our decision-making ability.

This also includes positions that are too large in relation to our account, and therefore possible losses that are too high given the consequences that we have just seen.

Position sizing is always essential to avoid this type of emotion.

General conditions

The pressure of everything that has to do with trading, or with our lives, emotional stress, particular moments of financial pressure, negatively affect us.

We may experience extended drawdown periods but still within the parameters of our strategy, and we must not be influenced by the fact that we have to pay the bills.

In the same way, moments of stress or difficulties of various kinds can happen in life, which have nothing to do with trading, but we must always be aware that we bring them in our way of trading, willingly or not.

Recognizing these situations and taking the necessary precautions not to change behavior is absolutely necessary.

Character

Many sides of one's character have influence on our trading: there are those who do not like to follow the rules, those who are impulsive, those who love excesses or taking risks.

All these are sides that can put our ability to be disciplined at risk.

For this reason it is important to know yourself, and choose a style of trading that is in line with ourselves, even exploiting perhaps these sides that may seem difficult to approach the trading, in any case trying to work simultaneously on improving their opposites.

The Deadly Habits In Trading

You access trading from many different life paths, often with the illusion of building a fortune, perhaps starting with few means and even in a short time.

There are no barriers to the entry of the Stock Exchange, so everyone can participate, from those who approach with caution and discipline to the gambler who simply sees another game of chance.

In between, dozens of poorly trained people are pulverized, along with their capital, often burning their accounts with trading habits that prove deadly and destructive.

Unfortunately, most people who approach trading take the destructive route because becoming a professional trader requires hundreds of hours of preparation and observation, while the general mentality sees the markets as a casino.

In reality, being profitable requires you to study your strategies for months or years and continue to perfect them.

And continuing to analyze your trading habits, changing them every time they get in the way.

But what are the 10 worst and most destructive trading habits for capital (material and psychological)?

Overtrading:

Each setup needs to be reflected in the set of rules that lead us to decide that it is valid, and that we can take that risk.

Instead very often, the adrenaline you feel when you are exposed to the market becomes the motivation main, leading to open positions just for the rush to win or lose.

This habit is particularly harmful if you come from a series of random winnings, i.e. that you do not depend on the strategy and how we followed it, and they make us feel invulnerable.

Follow the advice of others:

The best trades meet the necessary characteristics before entering the market.

This process takes a lot of effort, and leads less experienced traders to give up their jobs necessary and follow the advice of those who are considered to be more experienced, whether they are a bank manager, a trader on twitter or an FB group.

The riskiest thing is that not understanding the setup you enter with nor the strategy behind it (it is not you don't know what to do when things go wrong.

Lever too high:

Nowadays the leverage offered by brokers, both on cfd and also on Futures (although less in terms of margin) is high, and you need to learn as quickly as possible that it should not be used but you should use leverage.

If we use the margin we can, we will have an exposure to the risk of losing our capital very high, far beyond the capital itself.

Martingale:

Traders learn early on that they can lower their average loading price by adding more positions at a loss, at a "better" price.

Seems like a good idea, in fact it is increasing the risk to which you expose yourself, in a trade that is already and you can find yourself on the wrong side for weeks or months on the side wrong of the market, with an exposure at this point too high, and a capital that is being eroded.

Another matter if this mediating is foreseen by the strategy, and the total risk was calculated before, with criteria we haven't passed.

Follow the Sentiment:

Traders can choose to learn through a training process or follow the emotional response. In this case, the fear of losing the possible movement takes absolute control, attracting the trader in position at the worst possible time, when all others have already closed and led home the profit.

The need to be right:

If your real life is not going well, don't trade, because the problems in your personal life will bring blood and tears to your trading account.

This is especially true when you have decision-making problems, which raise an unhealthy desire to be right in all situations.

This subconscious force turns every operation into a referendum on one's self-esteem instead of just being a reasoned bet on whether a price will go up or down.

Betting on Quarterly:

During the period of profit exit, securities can move a lot during the closing of the market, as a reaction to quarterly results.

Beginner traders rely heavily on this type of movements, convinced that they can get to the wealth with betting results, instead of building it one piece at a time. On the contrary, part of the professionals remain out of these movements, unless to be able to reduce risks with option strategies.

Go against Trend:

We've always heard the motto "trend is your friend," even Gann used to say that in 1928, but still today the beginner does not hear this message, and tries to sell on new highs or buy on new minimum, without realizing that an absolute maximum or minimum is only defined as such afterwards.

In both cases, they fail to realize that a trend can last much longer than expected and go well beyond the price targets you thought.

Going countertrend is not bad, mind you, but even here there are some rules to follow, first and foremost not get an idea, but look at the facts.

Someone else is always to blame:

A bad habit is to always blame someone else for your losses, instead of to themselves.

Before they were the Market Makers today the HFT and the speculation of the Central Banks, the result is always the Same: Nobody but yourself comes to click on your mouse.

Do not have an exit plan:

If you don't have a trading plan, you don't know when to exit in profit or loss, and you risk to hold a position until you have an emotional crash, for better or worse.

This is incomprehensible to a professional, who would never go into an operation before having defined both potential loss and possible gain.

The 9 Fears Of Trading

Manage your emotions. This doesn't mean not having or not having emotions, that would be impossible.

For me it means living with them well, without being at their mercy and getting rid of negative moods.

Emotionality pushes us to extremes: euphoria, excitement / discouragement and fear are two sides of the same coin, and both prevent us from staying in balance, where calm, patience and prudence (the trader's paradise) reigns.

To simplify, I have to say that emotionality comes from fear: the fear of losing, of making mistakes, produces emotions that we perceive as negative, such as discouragement, but at the same time that same fear produces euphoria when it is denied by a position in gain.

When we trade with the risk of a real monetary loss, our lizard brain (limbic system) interprets it as a real danger to our biological survival.

And survival has completely to do with the emotional state we call fear.

Fear creates a lack of reactivity, a kind of box in which we are "well" and from which we prefer not to get out, since as we have seen it is created both a biological and psychological point of view from the survival mechanism, to avoid risks, therefore discomfort.

This "box" is made by our automatic reactions, which limit the possibilities, to see, to do, etc., is the famous Comfort Zone.

The 9 fears of trading

We can find 9 kinds of fears that manifest themselves in trading, and the interesting thing is that these fears existed within you even before you started trading, they were not born in trading, simply in other contexts you could avoid having to face them.

So let's start to give a name and get to know the demons that we keep inside, under the surface.

Fear of uncertainty

In trading it manifests itself as that little voice that, when we see a setup consistent with our trading plan, whispers to us "Are you sure? wait a moment, some other confirmation" and in the meantime we see the possible operation slip through our hands.

In trading we experience this kind of fear when we have a hesitation, when we wait to have a confirmation that a certain thing is going to happen; but in trading there are no certainties, only probabilities.

To get out of the biological mandate we have to manage the emotional state, to be able to overcome the imperative that we have impressed in the mind and body: we have to calm the brain, so that the fear of the uncertain does not overwhelm our rational thoughts, which are necessary to be able to put risk management into practice.

Fear of loss (of the click)

This is one of the most common fears. This is the moment of truth, when a trader understands if they are emotionally stable enough at a certain moment, when fear destroys the possibility of being in a state of calm, discipline and impartiality.

It is also the moment when one discovers how interconnected mind and body are, because both freeze with fear.

The mind is caught up in the expectation of imminent loss, all attention is focused on loss.

We create the loss ourselves, because we only see the possibilities that that emotional state allows us, and we lose the impartiality to see the setups as they are.

Managing this fear avoids the mental short circuit that prevents us from following the rules of risk management.

Fear based on the urgency to make up for previous losses

This type of fear often manifests itself as a mixture of anxiety and a sense of urgency, which takes away impartiality.

In the beliefs of many traders, there is no room to lose, it is a very remote possibility, probably due to the type of previous work or social environment.

The difference is the way to put yourself in front of the market: not to take from the market, but to see with a lot of open-mindedness if today can give us something good.

To become profitable and successful traders we must accept, but deep down, losses, and understand what they are. Now you know they'll be there.

You have to separate your performance from your identity as a person.

Afraid of being wrong or not being right.

If you are a perfectionist, until you have reorganized your knowledge of yourself, you will have a difficult time trading.

Even if you understand that you cannot always win in trading, on an emotional level you will remain attached to an unrealistic standard of perennial victories.

This mental attitude leads to a constant negative inner dialogue, of criticism of one's way of operating or not operating.

In trading, the success of a trade is not guaranteed just for doing it correctly, so excessive obsessive attention to perfection makes us less willing to see the constant change of the market.

A perfectionist attitude often hides the need for control and external validation of our work, but the market cannot be controlled, and is a dangerous place to put your sense of identity. You have to approach the market with respect for what you cannot control, which is everything but yourself, after all.

Fear of inadequacy (External validation)

If the need to provide subsistence becomes the need to prove your value and adequacy as a trader, this becomes a vulnerability in trading.

If you confuse performance with identity, then the need to have external validation of your value takes over.

If you develop a strong sense of yourself, of your essence, you can work on your performance, evaluate it painlessly, and develop more skills.

Fear of self-sabotage (sending everything into a state of flux)

Self-sabotage is a self-fulfilling prophecy, which we have wired into our neurocircuits, about our expectations for the future.

Fear of missing the chance (Greed)

Fear of missing an opportunity often leads to risk management, which keeps a trade within low, previously defined and acceptable risk parameters.

Sometimes it comes out without losses, if you have been smart enough but put the operation to breakeven, sometimes at a loss, but in any case given the gain before the psychological loss that we have suffered is considerable.

Greed drives out rationality, and the trader begins to see everything with the eyes of greed and opposition.

In trading, if we do not recognize this fear and learn how to manage it, it will burn our account.

We need to build the inner strength and discipline to resist the sirens of greed.

Fear of Failure/Fear of Success

In trading it can manifest itself in many ways, from not taking the risks that we had taken into account in our trading, keeping us out of the market, to closing a profitable trade too early, etc, etc...

What we have to do is take note that this mental attitude comes from far away, start to see it at work, and slowly change it, building new brain connections and new ways of dealing with things, and above all finally giving us permission to win, to succeed.

Fear of growth and change (getting out of the comfort zone box)

Each of us has a figure in mind that would put it right, both monthly and annually, but we must be careful not to turn it from an objective (which may even be exceeded) to an impassable wall, precisely because if we get there, we still risk losing what we have gained.

It can become the line in the sand that we have drawn for ourselves, that we cannot overcome, and also a self-fulfilling prophecy.

When attempting to re-examine our unconscious beliefs, we will find that many of the things that we believe, that we do not question, are not really "ours", we forged them in our neurons, and we accepted them because we certainly could not do anything else.

The 6 Most Common Emotions In Trading

Emotions in trading are undoubtedly among the most important factors and learning how to manage them is fundamental to becoming and remaining profitable in the long run.

A distinction must be made between emotions and feelings: emotions are energies that have a clear manifestation in the physical body (it is a great help to learn to recognize them), they are basically reactions to something that has not really happened (but for the human mind there is no difference).

When we are highly emotional, we are filled with a kind of energy that takes us away from our center, away from our inner clarity.

Our 'inner child' is the seat of our emotions. We know that children can get carried away with their emotions and are often unable to stop them, they can almost drown in their own emotions.

The 6 most common emotions in trading

Fear

Fear is one of the two most frequent emotions, it manifests itself in various ways and can be the cause of many trading errors.

Fear of losing causes traders to delay the moment of taking a loss, which then turns into much greater losses, and fear of giving back profits causes traders to close winning trades too soon.

Greed

Greed (a desire to increase one's "possession") would seem a good thing, but in reality it is often the cause of a series of impulsive trading decisions that should be avoided.

Traders who are influenced by greed often do not adhere to principles of sound risk and money management. Greed also reinforces the gambling mentality that leads to unregulated transactions made on the basis of impulsive decisions.

Hope

Hope, fear and greed often go hand in hand. Traders who have a position at a loss often show signs of hope when they delay making a loss and give a trade more room to breathe than they anticipated.

Another example of hope is when traders try to make up for past losses and then enter the market with an oversized position that does not follow their rules.

Agitation/ Anxiety

Every feeling of agitation in trading is a sign that something has gone wrong. When you are overly anxious when you are in a trade, it is often a sign that your position is too big, you have not followed the rules or that you should not have opened that trade.

Keeping track of your level of agitation and wondering why you are feeling anxious or agitated can often help you get out of trades you shouldn't have entered.

Boredom

Boredom is more a state of mind than an emotion, but traders who are bored often lack focus and clarity of mind. A sign of lack of attention is when you find yourself repeatedly looking at the charts of the same instruments and timeframes, without knowing what you are looking for.

Also, when you lose an entry due to lack of attention because you were surfing the Internet or doing something else is a sign that your focus is not where it should be.

Clarify your priorities and when you're operating, don't engage in other things.

Frustration

Frustration is also often the cause of trading errors, which result from any of the emotions we have talked about. When a trader loses an entry, breaks his rules and loses money, takes too many risks and loses too much money, and starts to see what he should have done, frustration starts to take over.

Frustration also reinforces all negative behavior patterns in a trader's activity by intensifying problems.

The Law Of Pareto In Trading

I guess you already know the Pareto Law or 80/20 Law:

"most effects are due to a small number of causes (considering large numbers)", which was then formulated as a model applicable in any field.

80% of your trading profits come from 20% of your trades.

The trick is therefore to focus on the essentials, learn to identify those few elements that really work, and eliminate what is useless, in particular dispersive or otherwise unproductive habits and behaviors.

The three problems that in general are responsible for most losses are:

Making mistakes that eat up all the profits

Traders can often be disciplined for several weeks in a row and perform very well.

Then, suddenly, something snaps in their mind and with just one trade they eliminate weeks of profits, usually mediating a position at a loss or enlarging (or worse, removing) the stop loss.

Here often a way to improve and solve this is to start keeping track of your mistakes, contextualizing them at all levels, in your emotional trading journal, so you can get statistics on their frequency and get to work on the more serious ones as results.

Turning profits into losses due to poor trade management

Once you enter the market, maybe well and according to your own rules, it can occur that a trader does not know what to do because they were only focused on entry, or that the rules of trade management are not properly followed because they're driven by the anxiety of the market.

Having a good trading plan, and following it, can improve these aspects.

Lever too high

Especially at the beginning, dreams of easy wealth leave many victims in the field, this is because if you don't carefully manage the level of risk you submit yourself to in every trade you make, the use of high leverage will quickly bring the account to zero.

Before you even start, it's best to study a little bit of Money Management, to get a clear understanding of both risk management and proper position sizing.

Small Final Suggestions

Success in trading is 80% psychology and 20% methodology

If the perfect trading system were published on the front page of the Wall Street Journal, only 10% of the people who applied it would be profitable, the rest would continue to lose money.

Why is that? The cause is lack of self-control and trust. From an early age we are used to gaining power to be able to manipulate and force change and follow our destiny. This is the only way we are taught to achieve our goals in life.

This right mental attitude does not work in the trading environment!

Manipulating the market is something beyond our capabilities and our control.

The only part of trading that we can control is ourselves.

How do you achieve self-control and trust?

Self-control is achieved through the exercise of discipline and the achievement of trust through the constant improvement of trading skills.

In the market, you and you alone must make the decisions - and you must have the discipline to share the decisions you make.

A trader has the power to give money to himself or to give his money to someone else.

In the trading environment, a trader will make his own decisions and therefore needs the discipline to be consistent with his own rules!

The question of statistics

As a trader are you willing to admit that your trading system is simply going through a period of losses?

Everyone goes through periods when our market entries generate consecutive losses - and then we start thinking...

It is the negative thoughts that negatively affect our confidence, which can also lead to big losses.

At the same time many traders who are just starting out will win. These winnings will erode the initial humility of these traders, as well as intensify their greed.

This is a very serious problem. Many traders have had to deal with these types of problems. Overcoming this kind of psychological barrier is crucial to a trader's success.

So, the lesson to learn is - Apply your rules!

Let's say that you start with a $5,000 account and risk a maximum of 1% of your balance in each single trade.

Using this strategy, you will have to fail 100 times in a row to clear your account.

Do you think it's likely to lose 100 times in a row? Only if you don't learn from your mistakes!

If you can conform your discipline to follow the rules of your trading system, you will have eliminated the dangerous "human factor" from your trading. This will really be an important step in becoming a trader of success.

Remember - don't keep your trading problems to yourself!

First of all, there are a few things we all need to understand, no matter where you are as a trader:

From a psychological point of view, the trading environment has the possibility to meet the wider expectations of financial independence and freedom, while, at the same time, there is also the possibility to risk everything you own in financial terms.

You, as a trader, will have to control yourself in a way that may be completely unknown to you, and this is no less absolutely essential for any kind of long-term success in this and similar markets.

The trading environment gives you the opportunity to experience complete freedom of expression combined with endless possibilities and risks.

How would a novice trader answer the following questions?

– Are you prepared to lose?

– Can you afford to lose?

– Do you, as a trader, always want to protect your capital?

Many traders convince themselves that they have found a safe trade, and therefore do not place any stop-losses, as the rule dictates.

Inevitably, they will have to juggle not to lose a large part of their capital.

This is an old story heard many, many times by the visitors to the Live Trading Room.

"I'm right, it's the market that's wrong!"

Many novice traders have the misconception that trading business happens naturally. They believe that they are the only ones who are qualified to succeed without studying and gaining experience.

The question of Drawdown

With a disciplined approach strictly following your rules, you won't need to search for the Holy Grail of input signals.

Keep your current system and make it your Holy Grail by breaking down the drawdown.

How do I lower my drawdown?

There are various strategies to trade with a limited drawdown.

For example the Probability Study when you can quite accurately identify the direction of the market in the next few hours and then execute orders in that direction.

As a result we will have, that even if our entry does not have perfect timing, just by having entered in the diagnosed direction, we will have a high-efficiency entry system and a decrease of the drawdown given by the decrease of consecutive losses.

You are the trading system

Many novice traders are in too much of a hurry and are impatient.

They have unrealistic expectations about making a pile of money quickly and in the short term.

This is the cause of breaking the rules (if they have any).

We probably get closer to the truth if we think that a good trading methodology alone will earn money.

You as a trader are the real trading strategy. You are the "Trading System"-and when you can combine a little patience with discipline to wait for the right moment, according to your guidelines and rules (even if you betray with only two moving averages) you will be on the right track.

Keep your trading clean!

If you're on the losing side, why don't you start exporting up to 1% of your capital per trade and keep track of your trades?

Remember that if you can decrease your drawdown you can expose yourself more at the end of the day to increase your profits.

However, you must keep your drawdown in order before proceeding to the next step.

(Almost like you have to take one step back first so you can take three steps forward.)

Cheating with Guidelines, Money Management and Psychology, these factors are definitely much more deeply important than it sounds. Don't kid yourselves!

Let's discuss Speculation

Speculating is to dedicate money in the hope of making an extraordinary profit, based on the assumption of risk and possible return associated with each individual trade.

Many of us are speculators. We use a series of strategies based on a set of rules and/or a number of indicators and then we scan currency pairs to capture profits from short-term movements.

That said, let's talk about the fabulous world of "gambling":

Gambling implies betting on uncertain success and accepting risk for the thrill of the game and accepting the verdict whether it has positive or negative returns.

Why do we have to keep this in mind? Doesn't it make you think that sometimes what all of us in the market are actually doing is gambling?

To be honest yes! Sometimes I make this interesting consideration.

Think about it this way-you pay money to acquire a method sold by professional traders and start trading, but it makes you lose money!

Why is this happening? Because you are in fact a gambler. Yes, dear friend, you are. Every single human being in this vast world is different.

Trading gurus who sell trading systems are part of the system and as they give you a method you don't do it the same way because you don't think the same way and at the same time you are gambling.

So, what do we learn from this?

"To become a successful trader, you must first become completely disciplined in what you do, before you think about taking a method from someone else and using it!"

Traders need an advantage, and it is logical to change from a gambler to a speculator with a good chance of winning.

Keep your market entry system, whatever it is, and execute it in a certain context.

For example, using the probability study, if only to remove consecutive losses.

Go check your transactions-every time an account is cleared, it happens when you suffer a series of consecutive losses. Betraying into a context removes these consecutive losses.

Forget the search for the Holy Grail, you are the Holy Grail.

Take back your losing strategy (market entry system) and turn it into your own. Performing only those high probability inputs, even if you don't immediately make a lot of money.

If you manage to reduce your consecutive losses, the money will go into your pockets time after time and only after you take your trades into account will you realize how much your withdrawal is.

After you know your drawdown, you can expose yourself in agreement, and make more profit at the end of the day.

To become a successful trader you must follow these steps first and reach your goals.

CONCLUSION

If you're reading the conclusion, it means you've reached the end of the book.

I hope it was a pleasant read and the information was interesting.

I hope, from all this, you learn to discover your real success in life. You will be able to find your talents and make the most of them, you will be able to combine a few small habits in life and in trading that will lead you to improve both. I'm sure that after reading this book, at the right time, you will be able to leapfrog into the pond and not into hot water!

I wish you every success in trading and other endeavours, have a great life!

Lightning Source UK Ltd.
Milton Keynes UK
UKHW022018101221
395433UK00010B/768